From Painting by L. A. Ramsey.

JOSEPH SMITH.

THE LATTER-DAY PROPHET

YOUNG PEOPLE'S
History of Joseph Smith

By GEORGE Q. CANNON

Fredonia Books
Amsterdam, The Netherlands

The Latter-Day Prophet:
Young People's History of Joseph Smith

by
George Q. Cannon

ISBN: 1-4101-0826-0

Reprinted from the 1914 edition

Fredonia Books
Amsterdam, The Netherlands
http://www.fredoniabooks.com

PREFACE TO FIRST EDITION.

In sending out this little work, the author hopes with all his heart that he has made interesting and instructive a subject that has been a source of inspiration to him. The book was called forth mainly by the need of the Sunday Schools for such a publication. In many schools the author's *Life of Joseph Smith* is being used, but that book was not written as a text-book for children. This little volume can be put to such a use, and can be placed in the hands of the children themselves. Teachers may gather new material to give them from any source they desire, but the children have a foundation furnished here.

In this book there may be words that a child of ten or twelve years will not understand; but a child's vocabulary would never grow if he met no new words. However, the author believes there are few if any places where an intelligent child cannot gather the meaning from the context. The work is purposely arranged in forty chapters, as that is the number of Sundays, fast-days excluded, in the year; but if possible, a little time once a month should be given to review work. Special attention is called to the chapter headings, which may be used as the topics on which different members of the class may prepare to talk. The maps and illustrations will be found valuable in aiding the child's understanding. While these suggestions apply to the use of this volume as a text-book, it has also been the aim to have the history suitable for general reading as well.

It has been the author's desire through life to aid in giving the young Latter-day Saints so much that is good and pure in literature that they will have no excuse for reading that which is trashy or improper. Good books, if not the strongest outside influence, are at least very strong in the building of character. The story of life upon the earth is beautiful, and has absorbing interest if that life is natural, that is, in harmony with the will of our Father in Heaven. The real experiences of a bold missionary of Truth should be and are of the highest interest to all right-minded "Mormon" children of either sex.

4 PREFACE.

Hence the author has seen fit to regard this little work as the beginning of a series of biographies of the Presidents of the Church, which he has under contemplation. He believes that the data of the history of the Church can be given as completely in the lives of the men who have led it as in any other way. There are some additional advantages: a biography has greater unity and consequently children can grasp it better, they obtain a deeper understanding, too, of the Church and its principles, when they see the life-history and growth of a man under the influence of the Gospel; and they become intimately acquainted with the noblest characters that have ever lived upon the earth. Besides this, the history of the Church is divided into periods that correspond with the time that each man has been President Each may almost be considered an epoch. The Church was organized and its members grew to be a strong people in the life of Joseph Smith; they became pioneers and colonizers in the life of Brigham Young; John Taylor's presidency was marked by the dark struggles which threatened the very existence of the Church itself. Wilford Woodruff's by the wonderful progress of the Saints when given liberty. Lorenzo Snow's already promises to mark a new and eventful period.

THE LATTER-DAY PROPHET is now sent forth, with the fervent prayer that it may create in the hearts of the children of Zion a great love for the man who made of human life a thing so nearly divine, and help them to go gravely forward with the work he was chosen to begin.

THE AUTHOR.

CONTENTS.

CHAPTER XI.

CHAPTER XII.

CHAPTER XIII.

CHAPTER XIV.

CHAPTER XV.

CHAPTER XVI.

CHAPTER XVII.

CHAPTER XVIII.

CHAPTER XIX.

CHAPTER XX.

8 CONTENTS.

THE LATTER-DAY PROPHET.

YOUNG PEOPLE'S
HISTORY OF JOSEPH SMITH.

CHAPTER I.
1805-20.

BIRTHPLACE OF THE PROPHET JOSEPH SMITH—HIS AN-
CESTORS—REMOVAL TO NEW YORK STATE—A RE-
LIGIOUS REVIVAL.

IT was two days before Christmas in the year eighteen
hundred and five, and cold winter had already set in.
The Green Mountains of Vermont were white with the
snow that had fallen, and now it lay also in the valleys
and upon the level land. It was the season when men
celebrate the birth of our Savior, and they felt in their
hearts the gladness and peace that come with Christmas tide.

Twenty miles east of the Green Mountains, on the
White River, a branch of the Connecticut, lies the little
town of Sharon. To a humble family living there, came
additional joy that day. A son was born, and, though
they knew it not, he was destined to be very great. He
was not the first-born, two sons and a daughter had

come before; but none the less did his parents welcome him. They gave him his father's name—Joseph Smith —a good name and never tarnished by an evil deed, but one to be known for both good and evil through all the world.

The boy came of goodly parentage. The Smiths, since Robert and Mary settled in Essex, Massachusetts, a century and a half before, had been honorable farmers. Lucy Mack, the mother, was also of a family of industrious land-owners. Members of both families had fought for their country. The father and mother of the boy, Joseph and Lucy, when they were married in 1796, and for a few years afterward, had been well-to-do, but had lost all in paying the debts brought upon them by the fraud of a trusted agent. They had left their home in Tunbridge, Vermont, and moved to Sharon in the adjoining county of Windsor. Here the father farmed in the summer and taught school in the winter. But little success came as the reward of his industry. He tried other places and at length, in the year 1815, he left the Green Mountain state entirely and moved his family to New York.

It seems as though the Lord must have had a hand in the misfortunes of Joseph Smith, Senior, and his wife Lucy. He was teaching them and their children humility. They all had their share of hard work and of the sacrifices that poverty brings. But hard work strengthened their bodies, and sacrifice strengthened their souls. They had no time to dream away their lives. They were taught rather to be industrious and to do their duty.

The father was a large, vigorous man, and the younger Joseph and his brothers inherited his strength. They worked at his side in the fields and helped him provide for the family wants. He taught them while at work, and when at rest by the fireside, to be truthful, honest and virtuous, and to love God. He gave them also lessons in reading and writing, but they had no such chance to learn these things as have children now-a-days.

The Lord doubtless directed the family in their journey westward to New York. It was there that His latter-day work must begin. Joseph, the instrument of that work, was nine years old at the time. The family first came to Palmyra, Wayne County, a little town lying twelve miles south of Lake Ontario. Here for about four years they labored in clearing the land and making themselves a home. Then they moved a mile or two south to Manchester, Ontario County, and took up land for a farm. There were now eight children in the family: Alvin, Hyrum, Sophronia, Joseph, Samuel, William, Catherine and Don Carlos.

In the second year after they had come to Manchester the Methodists of that region began a religious revival. The Presbyterians and Baptists soon joined. A revival is caused by holding frequent meetings where those who attend preach, sing and pray, and try by all means to stir up religious enthusiasm. Sometimes they go to great extremes, and scream and groan and dance until nearly exhausted. These actions are of course not directed by the Spirit of the Lord. In Manchester there was great excitement and many were converted, or at least joined themselves with one or other of the sects. As the people began to divide up, much strife arose, and so much bad feeling was shown that one could hardly believe they were true followers of Jesus.

CHAPTER II.

1820.

JOSEPH was fourteen years old at the time of the revival. He was large for his age and inclined to be serious in his thoughts. With the other members of his family he took great interest in religion, and felt it his duty to join some church and thereby be saved. But which church should he join? That was very hard for the boy to answer. The other members of the family decided that the Presbyterians were right, and the mother, with Hyrum, Samuel, and Sophronia joined their church. This made Joseph very uneasy, because he was inclined to believe with the Methodists, and the feeling between these two sects was very bitter.

His mind became greatly excited sometimes, for he felt that he ought to do something to gain salvation, and yet he could not decide what was right to do. He felt sure that all the churches could not be true, for if they were they would unite to help each other instead of trying to do each other harm. He thought that he should not join any church until he knew the right one, and so he waited.

Joseph was only fourteen years old and did not have a good education, but he could read the Bible and could understand many of the truths written there. He made a practice of comparing the teachings of the ministers that were seeking to convert him with the teach-

ings of Jesus and His Apostles.   This made him all
the more doubtful, for he saw that they did not entirely
agree.

He was certainly in great difficulty, but he per-
severed and at last found a way out.   In his Bible he
came upon a passage that was written for him and for
all who need light. It is the first chapter of the Apostle
James' epistle to the Saints, the fifth verse: "If any
of you lack wisdom, let him ask of God, that giveth
to all men liberally, and upbraideth not; and it shall be
given him."   Those words sank deep into his heart.
He thought them over again and again, and at length
made up his mind to obey them and pray for wisdom.
In the sixth and seventh verses James tells that we
must not waver if we wish to receive anything from the
Lord. Joseph probably read these verses, too, for when
he made up his mind to seek wisdom he was full of
hope that the Lord would hear him.

It was morning, early in the spring of 1820.   The
sky was clear, the air cool and refreshing, and all was
beautiful. Green woods surrounded the home of Joseph,
and to them he took his way alone.   He found a suitable spot and looked around to make sure that no one
was near.   Then he kneeled down, and for the first
time in his life sought the Lord in vocal prayer.

He had barely begun when an unseen power seized
him and made him speechless.   All grew frightfully
dark, and he felt as though he were about to be destroyed. He realized that it was the awful power of
the evil one, and he called on God to save him.   But
his strength was fast giving way and sickening despair
was taking possession of him, when a pillar of divine
light appeared above him and the prince of darkness
fled.

The light descended, and within it Joseph beheld

two radiant beings, too glorious and beautiful to be described. They looked just alike to him and appeared to have equal splendor and authority, until one of them, pointing to the other, said, "JOSEPH, THIS IS MY BELOVED SON, HEAR HIM."

The humble boy was almost overcome by the glory of the vision before him, and he could not at once continue his prayer for light. But the kindliness and love of the Father and of the Lord Jesus gave him assurance and he was at length able to speak. He asked which church was right that he might join it, and even in the glory of the vision he was surprised, for the divine instruction came that all were wrong.

Jesus said that all their creeds were an abomination in His sight; that those professors were all corrupt; they drew near Him with their lips, but their hearts were far from Him; they taught for doctrine the commandments of men, having a form of godliness, but they denied the power thereof. He told Joseph that he should join none of them, but at some future time the true Gospel would be revealed to him. Other words of comfort and wisdom were spoken, and then the vision withdrew.

When Joseph came to himself he was lying on the ground looking up into heaven. He was filled with a spirit of peace and joy, for now he knew that he would yet be taught how he might save his soul. He knew that God and Jesus were living beings with bodies which his own resembled. He knew that they sympathized with him, and loved him, and oh, how intensely did he love them! He rose and returned home feeling that he had a glad message for mankind, which they would rejoice to hear.

HOW THE ACCOUNT OF HIS VISION WAS RECEIVED—HIS
FURTHER INQUIRY FOR LIGHT—ANOTHER VISION.

FOR many centuries no person on earth had asserted that he had seen and spoken with heavenly beings. People had almost forgotten that visions and the ministering of angels had any part in human life. When a country-bred lad declared that he had been visited by our Father in heaven and His Son Jesus, the Creators of this earth and its inhabitants, the people were astonished. Without thinking of the matter seriously or seeking to find a cause for such bold words, they immediately set them down as false, though the boy before this had been known to be honest and truthful.

Some that heard his words feared they might be true, and since they did not love the truth, sought to destroy it by ridicule and persecution. A Methodist minister, who had taken much interest in Joseph on account of his earnestness, was one of the first to whom the boy gave an account of what he had seen. This man must have had less faith in God's power than in Satan's, for he told Joseph that the vision was from the devil. He said that since the Apostles there had been no revelations from God; these things had ceased forever.

Joseph knew that he had seen a glorious vision. He could not deny it, for in doing so he knew he would grievously offend God. Though only a boy he was reviled and persecuted by all classes of men. The ministers of the different churches sought especially to make life bitter for him, and the members of his family suffered with him. Joseph's pious friends of former days became his enemies and he had to seek new associations. He says that these were sometimes not the best company, and he fell into many foolish errors.

Three and a half years passed, and Joseph was nearly eighteen years old. The thought began to grow in his mind that he ought to learn how he stood before the Lord. He had often felt sorry for his wrong doing and wished to seek forgiveness. The summer of 1823 had closed and autumn had begun when Joseph decided that he would again ask for light. On the evening of the 21st of September, after he had gone to bed, he began to pray. He felt certain that an answer would come, for the prayer was from his heart. He had not finished before the darkness began to disappear. The humble bed-chamber was soon ablaze with wondrous light, and in the midst he saw an angel.

The form of the messenger was that of a tall and stately man. His head and neck were bare, and a graceful robe of lustrous white hung nearly to his naked ankles. The majesty of his form was increased by the exquisite beauty of his face, which shone like lightning. He stood near the bed-side but touched neither ceiling, walls nor floor. It was a spiritual sight; nothing on earth could approach it.

When Joseph's momentary fear had passed away, the angel, calling him by name, began his message. He said that he was Moroni, and that he had been sent from the presence of God. He told Joseph that his sins were forgiven and that God had a great work for him to do. This work would cause his name to be known for good or for evil among all nations, kindreds and tongues. He spoke of a record engraved on plates of gold and hidden in a nearby hill, that gave the history of the former inhabitants of this land and contained the fullness of the Gospel.   He described the Urim and Thummim—those two strange, transparent stones set in silver bows and fastened to a golden breastplate—and said that God had prepared them to be used in translating the record.

Then the heavenly visitor began quoting from the ancient prophets and apostles passages that referred to the last days, when the Priesthood was to be restored, the Holy Spirit to be poured out on all flesh, and peace and love were to reign on earth.   Some he quoted just as they are in the Bible, but he changed others, making them more plain.   He told Joseph of things that the boy could not mention afterward, because they were too holy.   He commanded him not to show the plates, Urim and Thummim or breastplate, when he received them, to any person except when commanded to do so by the Lord.   The vision of the hill was opened to Joseph's mind, while the angel spoke, and he distinctly saw just where the record was hidden.

Then the light withdrew from other parts of the room, but became more bright about the messenger and extended in a glowing path up into heaven.   Thither he ascended, darkness returned, and Joseph was left to wonder and rejoice.   Soon the light appeared again and the vision was repeated just as before.   Moroni added a prophecy of the terrible judgments that were coming on earth, of hunger, bloodshed and disease, and once more he rose heavenward.   It seemed necessary that Joseph should be deeply impressed with the message, and for the third time it was given him.   Each part was gone over with the same care as when given first.   The last words of the angel were a caution that he should never use the plates, when he received them, except to glorify God and build up His Kingdom.

2

The vision closed, and almost immediately the cocks began to crow. Soon the autumn morning dawned, and though Joseph had not closed his eyes in sleep, he arose to begin the labors of the day.

CHAPTER IV.

1823.

THE MORNING VISION—JOSEPH TELLS HIS FATHER— VISITS CUMORAH—THE PLATES FOUND—MORONI'S COMMAND.

JOSEPH went to work with his father that morning as if nothing had happened. He did not speak of the vision, though that doubtless was uppermost in his mind. Perhaps he thought that new persecution might be aroused and he would not spread the news of this visit of a heavenly being unless necessary. He could not work with his usual vigor, however, for his strength seemed to be gone. His father noticed that he was unwell and sent him home. Joseph set out, but in trying to cross the fence around the field he fainted and fell to the ground.

When he became conscious, the angel Moroni in glory was again at his side, and for the fourth time the entire vision was passed over. The angel then directed Joseph to go and tell his father all that had happened, and disappeared. Joseph returned and did so.

The father was probably much surprised to hear of the angel's visits and of his message. He had little dreamed that at the surface of the high hill within his sight were hidden sacred objects of priceless value, that among them were writings which the wisest men could but imperfectly understand, and that his unlearned son should be the guardian of these and by the power of God was to bring forth a perfect translation of them. But the father knew his boy and believed him. The inspiration of the Holy Spirit rested on him and he told Joseph that the vision was of God and that he should go and do as the angel had commanded him.

Joseph's strength returned somewhat and he set out for the hill to find the sacred record. The distance was only two and a half miles, so that the walk was not very long, but on the way he was sorely tempted to take the plates and use them for himself. The promptings of the Holy Spirit were still with him, however, and he overcame this evil thought.

On the west side of the hill, near the summit, he found the rounded top of a stone above the ground, and when he dug away the earth he saw that it was the cover of the box. This stone was somewhat in the shape of a shield with the outside upward, and when the earth covered the edges it looked like the top of an ordinary bowlder. Joseph had seen this exact spot in his vision and did not doubt that he would find the plates below, but his heart beat fast when he put his lever under and began to pry up the cover. He raised it without great difficulty and worked it off, and then within his reach he beheld the hidden treasure of gold.

Perhaps this boy had never read of the wondrous caves of Aladdin and Ali Baba, or of the secret treasures of Monte Cristo Island, but every boy has dreams of treasure-trove and of becoming rich and powerful. Whether Joseph was dazzled by the rich prize before him and for the moment thought this was just a dream come true, or whether he merely wished to examine these beautiful, strange things, we do not know, but he reached forth to draw them out. Immediately their guardian appeared and prevented him. The angel told him the time had not yet come for him to receive them. He must return on that same day, the 22nd of September, every year for four years, when, if he should be faithful, they would be given over into his care. This conversation occurred September 22nd, 1823. Until the four years were passed they should remain secure in their stone box.

Moroni told Joseph that he had hidden up the records four centuries after the birth of Jesus, while he was living on the earth. He said that the Nephites, the people to whom he belonged, called the hill where they stood Cumorah, and that a still earlier people, the Jaredites, called it Ramah. This was a very important hill in the history of both these peoples.

Joseph learned many other things that were new to him, and how strange he must have felt when he realized that he was the only person on earth to know them! While Moroni was still present, Joseph saw in vision the glory of God's kingdom and the horror of Satan's. The angel told him these had been shown that he might know the good from the evil and never be influenced or overcome by Satan's power.

When the vision was ended Joseph replaced the stone, covered it as before and returned home. That night when he retired to bed, he thanked the Lord for what He had taught him, and prayed humbly that he might keep himself pure and faithful. During the last twenty-four hours he had been visited five times by an angel of light, he had seen a great golden book, the history of the peoples that had passed away, and with the book, the holy seer-stone and the breastplate of gold. Besides all this his life-work had been shown him, and he now knew something of what he must suffer and what he must do.

———

CHAPTER V.
1824-27.

THE FOUR YEARS OF WAITING—JOSEPH WORKS IN PENN-
SYLVANIA—MARRIAGE—THE LAST VISIT TO THE
HILL—OUTRUNS THE ROBBERS.

FOR two years after this second great vision, Joseph labored at ordinary work, sometimes on his father's farm, other times as hired help away from home. His father and brothers also worked hard and through their industry were able to live comfortably. Alvin, Joseph's oldest brother. died in November, 1824, and this was a sad blow for the young Prophet, for Alvin constantly comforted him in persecution and rejoiced in the work he was to do. If he had lived he would have been as brave and steadfast as was Hyrum, but he died, and in dying gave Joseph a brother's blessing.

In October, 1825, Joseph left home and went to work for Josiah Stoal in what was said to be an old Spanish silver mine. It was situated in Harmony, Sus-quehanna County, near the northern border of the State of Pennsylvania. After digging uselessly for a month Joseph induced his employer to stop the work, for he saw it was only a waste of labor. Mr. Stoal had grown to like this tall, clear-headed youth and continued to employ him.

Joseph boarded, while at Harmony, with Isaac Hale, and while living there, fell in love with Mr.

Hale's daughter Emma. She was a worthy girl of high character, and they became engaged. There are some girls that have not enough love within them to marry a man unless he is rich or popular, or at least approved of by their friends or relatives; but Emma Hale was not of this class. Joseph was poor, and did not have a home of his own. He was persecuted also, and Emma's family objected to her marrying a man who had so many enemies. But she knew he was a manly man and believed him a chosen servant of God; she loved him and was willing to leave a comfortable home and live in poverty among strangers with him. They went to Squire Tarbill, at South Bainbridge, New York, to be married, and Joseph, leaving Mr. Stoal's employ, went home to Manchester to work with his father.

The marriage occurred January 18, 1827, less than a month after Joseph's twenty-first birthday. He was a man now and the time was drawing near when he should receive the plates. As Moroni commanded him, he had gone each year to Cumorah and had seen the contents of the stone box. The angel had taught him a great deal on each visit and had encouraged him to do right.

On September 22, 1827, the four years of waiting ended, and for the fifth time Joseph went to the hill. This time he opened the box, and Moroni, who had watched over it for fourteen hundred years, gave him the plates, the Urim and Thummim and the breastplate. The angel told him that he must guard them with his life, if necessary, and if he lost them through carelessness the Lord would reject him. Moroni warned him that wicked men would try as hard as they could to get the plates from him, but if Joseph did his best to keep them the Lord would help him.

The plates were about eight inches wide and each one was thinner than common tin.   There were so many, however, that it made a book about six inches thick.   All the sheets were bound together by three golden rings that passed through one edge, and three smaller rings fastened the other edge of about one-third, so that this part was sealed.   Each sheet was engraved on both sides with small beautiful characters, but they were very strange and not at all like anything Joseph had seen before.

The breastplate was of pure gold as were the plates.   This was made to cover the bosom of a large man and four golden straps extended from the corners for the purpose of fastening it to the body.   The Urim and Thummim was attached to the breastplate though it could be removed.   The Urim and Thummim was like a large pair of spectacles with silver bows and, instead of glasses, clear stones.

Joseph examined these beautiful things and was glad that the Lord had entrusted them to him, but he felt, too, that it was a great responsibility.   He had learned much during the past four years and knew that the possession of the plates would not increase his worldly pleasures.   He placed the treasures under his coat and, full of determination to protect them, he set out for home.   On the way wicked men tried to rob him; they struck him with a heavy club; but Joseph was a tall, strong man and a swift runner, and he escaped.   They chased him almost to his father's house without overtaking him, although he was handicapped by the great weight that he carried.

CHAPTER VI.

1827-28.

PERSECUTION—MARTIN HARRIS COMES TO JOSEPH'S AID
—ANTHON FULFILLS A PROPHECY—MARTIN BE-
COMES SCRIBE—STRANGE BOOK-WRITERS.

THE spirit of lying, robbery, and murder is awful
when it comes upon men, for it makes them seek
to destroy the truth and to hinder the work of God.
Mobs filled with this spirit were aroused against Joseph.
They continually sought to steal the holy plates, and in
doing this they would willingly have murdered him, but
he was very careful and the Lord helped him. Ministers, who ought to have been teaching the people to
be honest and pure, were most prominent in spreading
lies and stirring up hate against the young Prophet. He
had never harmed them, but he had been brave enough
to declare that the Lord had spoken to him, though the
world turned his enemy.

Moroni had directed Joseph to translate the record,
but his enemies were so cunning and so violent that he
had to hide it to keep it out of their hands. At one time
they would suddenly break into the house and tear up
the hearth, at another they would climb into the attic
and search; but in every case Joseph had removed the
treasure before they came, and they hunted in vain.
This of course kept him from translating, and at length
he decided that he would leave Manchester and go to
his wife's home in Pennsylvania, hoping to be able to
work there in peace. Joseph had received low wages
while working for Mr. Stoal and the year of farming
had not brought him much money. But Harmony,

where Mr. Hale lived, was about one hunred and fifty miles from Manchester and it was impossible for him to move without aid.

Sometimes the Lord inspires men to do strange things to help His work. Martin Harris, a well-to-do farmer, came to Joseph at this time, and in spite of all the lies he had heard, gave him fifty dollars. Joseph was now able to reach Pennsylvania. On the way, there was some excitement, for twice men came with search warrants and hunted for the plates. These were hidden in a barrel of beans and the men who would have liked to steal them failed.

It was December when he came to the home of his father-in-law, and for two months he worked at copying the characters from the plates to sheets of paper, and writing beneath the translation made by means of the Urim and Thummim. In February, 1828, Martin Harris came down to Pennsylvania and Joseph gave him the sheets. Martin took them to New York City to find out whether the characters would be accepted as real by learned men.

He showed them first to Professor Charles Anthon of Columbia College. Mr. Anthon examined them carefully and said that the translation was correct and the best he had ever seen of Egyptian characters. He wrote a certificate to this effect, and gave it to Martin. He asked how the young man happened to find the plates, and when Martin said that an angel had shown him where they lay, he asked for the certificate again. Martin returned it and Mr. Anthon tore it to pieces, saying that there was no such thing as the ministering of angels.

Although Mr. Anthon was too cowardly to let his name go before the public connected with what an angel was said to have revealed, yet he would have liked to obtain worldly praise by translating the record himself, and asked Martin to bring it to him. When told that this could not be done and that part of it was sealed, he replied, "I cannot read a sealed book." If you read the twenty-ninth chapter of Isaiah you will find that the prophet spoke of this circumstance two thousand five hundred years ago.

Martin Harris carried the characters to Dr. Mitchell, another learned man, and he also said they were genuine. This convinced Martin, and he returned to Pennsylvania. He now arranged with Joseph to become his scribe and to write at his dictation, but first it was necessary to return home that he might prepare for a long stay. He came back to Harmony about the middle of April ready to work.

Joseph had very little education at this time; he could not spell so well as the ordinary school-boy can now; his time had been spent in work, and he had had few oportunities to learn. But now a book lay before him written long ago in a strange tongue and he was to translate it into English. Isaiah said that the sealed book should be given to one that was not learned, and that certainly had now been done. Joseph could not take honor to himself as the traslator of it; he was only a humble instrument in the hands of God in bringing it forth.

When Martin came the second time he immediately began service with Joseph, and no writer of books ever worked as did they. A screen divided the room in which they sat. On one side of this was the young Prophet—a tall, manly fellow, dressed in working clothes that had seen long use, his serious, handsome face bronzed by the sun and wind, and his hands hardened by toil. Before him lay a pile of golden leaves in book form worth a fabulous sum from a worldly standpoint, and yet too sacred to be looked on even, except by the one chosen to bring them forth. Before his eyes he held large spectacles with thick, bright stones as glasses. Slowly he read aloud in simple English from the strange figures on the metal pages. On the other side sat a somewhat older man, well-dressed, but plainly a country-man, busily writing down the words that were spoken.

CHAPTER VII.

1828-29.

MARTIN HARRIS IMPATIENT—THE MANUSCRIPT LOST— GOD'S WISDOM SHOWN—JOSEPH REPENTS—SLOW PROGRESS OF TRANSLATION.

JOSEPH and Martin worked together until the translation covered one hundred and sixteen pages of foolscap paper. Martin Harris was not a patient man and it occurred to him that he would like to show his friends what he had written without waiting until the work was completed. Joseph refused to permit this, for the work was not done to gratify curiosity; but Martin teased and Joseph inquired of the Lord. The answer forbade Joseph's letting the manuscript go, but Martin was not satisfied and worried him until he asked again. Once more the Lord refused, and for a time Martin worked along without complaining; but his wife and other members of his family desired to see what was written of the new book, and he again induced Joseph to ask.

It was wrong for the Prophet to give way after the Lord had twice answered him, but Martin made so many promises to be careful that there seemed little reason for fearing injury to the manuscript. The last time the Lord replied that Martin might take the writings on condition that he would show them only to five persons, his wife, father and mother, brother and sister-in-law. Joseph, too, was held responsible for them. With very solemn vows Martin Harris covenanted to guard the writings and return them, but he was tempted to show them to other persons and they were stolen from him. They fell into the hands of evil men and neither he nor Joseph ever saw them again.

The Urim and Thummim had been taken from the Prophet because he displeased the Lord in asking so often about the writings. When Martin had gone from Harmony, after two months of work as scribe, Joseph went to his father's home on a visit being unable to go on with the work. He soon returned from Manchester and the Urim and Thummim was given back to him. He was permitted to keep it while the Lord gave him a revelation, and then it with the plates was taken away. Do not think that the Lord could not have given the revelation without the Urim and Thummim. In later years Joseph did not use it, but he was still young and the Lord perhaps thought it best to make him feel dependent by not communing openly at all times with him.

The revelation was a rebuke to him for his weakness and a warning that though he had been much favored he would still be rejected if he were not faithful and humble. The Lord told him that the work should still go on, even though he proved faithless. Joseph's sensitive spirit was deeply hurt and he humbly repented of what he had done.

The plates and the Urim and Thummim were

given back to him again and he was directed to continue his labors. It was revealed that if he should re-translate what Martin Harris had lost, those who had stolen the manuscript would change it in places and would deceive the world by saying that Joseph could not translate twice alike, and therefore his work was not of God. But though Satan had laid a cunning plot, the wisdom of God triumphed.

If you have read the Book of Mormon you have perhaps noticed a difference in the books of First Nephi, Second Nephi, Jacob, Enos, Jarom and Omni, from what follows. If you have not read this beautiful record, remember to notice the difference when you do, and you will see one sign of the complete wisdom and forethought of God. These books were written on the small plates of Nephi, and when Mormon, the father of Moroni, found them, he joined them to the abridgment he had made of the larger plates. The two sets of plates cover the same period of history, but the larger set deals more with government and the political affairs, while the smaller is rather a record of the dealings of the Lord with the people.

Nephi hardly knew why he was commanded by the Lord to make the smaller plates and write upon them, but he obeyed. Moroni tells us he did not know why he was moved upon to add them to his abridgement. But we now see the purpose of the Lord in it. The translation that Martin Harris lost was from Mormon's abridgment of the larger plates. Joseph was commanded to translate the same part from the smaller plates, and thus Satan's plan to deceive could not be used. This change makes the Book of Mormon more valuable, too, because on the smaller plates were written many choice prophecies and revelations that Mormon did not give in the abridgment.

Joseph did not at once begin to translate, but for a time worked on a small farm he had bought from his wife's father, Isaac Hale. He receved a number of important revelations about this time for the comfort and instruction of himself and of others who came to him. When he began to translate again, the work went on very slowly for he had no one to write for him regularly. Sometimes his wife Emma could spare time and a little progress was made. But Joseph and Emma had lost their firstborn child, a son, soon after his birth in July, 1828, and the mother through grief and poor health could give but little assistance in the work. This state of affairs continued until April, 1829.

CHAPTER VIII.

1829.

OLIVER COWDERY BECOMES SCRIBE—JOSEPH AND OLIVER PRAY FOR NEW LIGHT—THE PRIESTHOOD RESTORED—THE FIRST BAPTISMS—KINDNESS OF JOSEPH KNIGHT.

JOSEPH was now twenty-three years old, and his life up to this time had been in a sense only a preparation for his work. He had held the plates for a year and a half and though he had studied them and had translated a considerable part yet through Martin Harris' sin he was still at the beginning of the book. But that time had been valuable for him, though he had little to show for it. He had learned what the displeasure of the Lord means, and, though forgiven, he had been taught a lesson that he never forgot. Still he had been true to his trust in guarding the plates and no mortal eyes except his own had looked upon them.

As the sun was setting on Sunday, April 5, 1829, a young man came into Harmony and sought Joseph for the purpose of making his acquaintance and helping him. This man was Oliver Cowdery, who during the past winter had taught school at Manchester and, as teachers in country schools used to do, he boarded around at the students' homes. In these visits he came to live with the family of Joseph Smith, Senior, and there he heard of the younger Joseph and his work. He was at first struck by the strangeness of it all, and then prayed seriously to God to learn whether He really had revealed Himself in this day. The Holy Ghost manifested to him that Joseph had assuredly been visited by celestial beings and that he was called to aid the young Prophet in his work.

When school had closed, therefore, Oliver came to Pennsylvania, and two days after meeting Joseph the young men set themselves earnestly to the work of translation. There were few interruptions and as Oliver was used to writing the progress was rapid. Sometimes they found things in the Book of Mormon or the Bible that they did not understand although they talked them over together and studied them ever so hard, and when this happened they asked the Lord to explain these matters to them. Sometimes they prayed just as we do, and sometimes Joseph put on the Urim and Thummim besides; but the Lord always answered them and showed them what they did not understand.

When tired of writing they would often go for a walk in the woods or down to the river for recreation and healthful exercise. A favorite pastime was to throw stones into the stream. Joseph especially was very fond of jumping and wrestling, and was expert at both. It is said that he could walk under a pole—he was six feet tall—and then, taking a step or two back, jump over it. He was a noted wrestler, and in later life even, he often enjoyed a vigorous bout. Though his life was a most busy one he still found time to keep his body strong and healthy and to relax his mind by athletic practice.

About a month after beginning work, Joseph translated from the plates a passage that spoke of baptism. It said that it is necessary to be baptized in order that a person's sins may be washed away and forgiven. Neither Joseph nor Oliver had been forgiven of past sins by baptism, and after talking over the matter earnestly, on the fifteenth of May, 1829, they went into the woods to pray for light. While they were kneeling a voice from the midst of heaven bade them have peace, then the veil parted and John the Baptist came down before them. This is the same brave prophet who preached repentance and the coming of the Savior, in the wilderness of Judea, and baptized Him in Jordan. John was beheaded while in prison by Herod, but now he came quickened and clothed with glory.

He calmed them with his gentle yet thrilling voice, telling them he was their fellow-servant and acting under the direction of Peter, James and John. He laid his hands upon their heads and ordained them to the Aaronic Priesthood, which he represented in life. His words were:

"Upon you my fellow servants, in the name of Messiah, I confer the priesthood of Aaron, which holds the keys of the ministering of angels and of the gospel of repentance and of baptism by immersion for the remission of sins; and this shall never again be taken from the earth until the sons of Levi do offer again an offering unto the Lord in righteousness."

John then directed Joseph to baptize Oliver and that Oliver should baptize Joseph; after this in the same way they should ordain each other to the Aaronic Priesthood. He said that they must not lay on hands for the gift of the Holy Ghost as that was not the power of the Priesthood of Aaron. Later the Melchizedek Priesthood would be given them and then they could lay on hands and perform other holy offices.

There was a river near by and Joseph and Oliver went into it together, prepared to perform the sacred ordinance. It was a strange sight on earth, and no doubt the hosts of heaven were glad, for since the righteous Nephites no man had been cleansed from sin in the waters of baptism. Joseph seriously spoke the simple words of the ordinance and then laid Oliver beneath the water. As he drew him up, suddenly the spirit of prophecy came upon Oliver. He was filled with joy and foretold glorious things that were about to come to pass. Oliver then baptized Joseph and the Holy Spirit fell in a like manner upon him. He prophesied concerning the rise of the Church and of its progress, and declared many things that were to happen in that generation.

Filled with these exalted feelings Joseph laid his hands upon Oliver's head and ordained him a Priest after the order of Aaron, and Oliver did the same to Joseph. They already held the Priesthood, because that was given by John, but they re-ordained each other as a pattern for others, since the Priesthood was to be conferred in the future after baptism.

From this time on, the minds of the young men were enlightened and they understood things that had been mysteries before. Persecution had begun, and for a time they said nothing about what had taken place; but soon they began explaining the scriptures to all who would listen.

Joseph's brother Samuel, who came on a visit at this time, was shown the translation already made, and heard the testimony of Joseph and Oliver. After a time he became partially converted and went alone to pray and learn from the Lord whether the work was true. A strong testimony was given him, and soon after Oliver baptized him. On coming out of the water he too began to prophesy remarkable things, as Oliver and Joseph had done. Samuel returned home and Hyrum came to Harmony. He heard the truth and believed.

A very kind service was done the Prophet at this time by Joseph Knight, an old gentleman living in Broome County, New York. Now and at other times, he brought a load of provisions in order that Joseph and Oliver might keep on translating. But though supplied with food and protected from violence by the family of Isaac Hale, still persecution grew very severe against them and it seemed necessary to move from Harmony, if they wished to work in peace.

CHAPTER IX.

1829.

DAVID WHITMER TAKES THE PROPHET TO FAYETTE—
MANY BELIEVE AND ARE BAPTIZED—ELEVEN WIT-
NESSES SEE THE PLATES AND BEAR RECORD—THE
HIGHER PRIESTHOOD RESTORED—THE TRANSLATION
FINISHED.

EARLY in June, 1829, a young man drove up to Joseph's door after two days of hard traveling. He said that he had come from Fayette, Seneca Co., New York, one hundred and fifty miles away, for the purpose of carrying the Prophet and his companion to Fayette if they wished to go. He was David Whitmer, son of Peter Whitmer, and his father invited Joseph to come to their home. They offered him protection and to provide for his wants while he was working at the translation.

Joseph accepted the invitation and, leaving Emma with her father, he and Oliver departed with David. Before setting out Joseph asked the Lord how he should carry the plates. In answer to his prayer Moroni appeared and took them from him, promising to return them again. When he reached Fayette the angel visited him in Mr. Whitmer's garden and gave them over to him.

The translation continued very rapidly, for when Oliver grew tired, David or his brother John was ready to write at the Prophet's dictation. When not translating, Joseph and Oliver spent their time in teaching those who came to listen and in explaining what the Lord had revealed to them.

There were many serious persons who wished to hear the truth. David Whitmer had been remarkably aided that he might hasten to bring Joseph to Fayette. Three strange men were seen scattering the plaster that David had put in a heap upon one of his fields to fertilize it, and they did it with more than human skill and speed. In harrowing in wheat on another field David had done in one day more than he could usually have done in two or three days. Many in the neighborhood hearing of this were impressed that the Lord had helped him in bringing the two young men and believed that they were His servants.

When any person became convinced that the work was divine and desired to be baptized, the ordinance was performed. Joseph soon had the pleasure of baptizing his brother Hyrum and David Whitmer, and at the same time Oliver baptized Peter Whitmer, Junior. Soon there were so many believers that baptisms were performed nearly every day in Seneca lake, a beautiful body of water lying on the western border of Seneca County.

While at work on the translation it was learned that three persons should be shown the sacred plates, in order that their testimony might be given to the world. Oliver Cowdery, David Whitmer and Martin Harris begged Joseph to ask the Lord if they could not be the ones. Joseph did this during the month of June, 1829, and the Lord answered that if they trusted in His words with full purpose of heart they should be shown the plates, the breastplate, Urim and Thummim, sword of Laban and the Liahona, or compass, given to Lehi in the wilderness. Soon after they all went into the woods to pray that the Lord would show the plates, which Joseph had given up for the time to the Angel Moroni.

The four men kneeled down and Joseph offered a prayer, then the others in turn prayed, but no answer came. Joseph began again and the others followed but though they prayed with fervor yet they failed to receive any manifestation. Before beginning again Martin Harris said he believed he was the cause of the failure. He offered to go aside and pray alone.

Martin had spoken the truth, for soon after he withdrew, a light of surpassing fairness came down from heaven and within it stood the angel holding the golden plates. He turned the leaves and the characters engraved thereon were illumined so that the witnesses saw them plainly. They also heard the voice of the Lord declaring that the plates before them were revealed by God and had been translated by His power.

They were commanded to bear record that the translation was correct.

When the vision passed away Joseph sought Martin Harris. He found him, humbled by this rebuke for his past wickedness and praying with his whole heart for forgiveness and for the privilege of viewing the record. Joseph joined him in prayer and soon the angel again appeared and the whole vision was repeated. Martin had never beheld a spiritual sight before and he could not long bear the glory before him, but he was filled with joy and shouted hosanna to God.

The three men who had been chosen as witnesses drew up and signed a statement, which is now printed in the fore part of the Book of Mormon. They testified to all the world that they had seen an angel holding the plates and heard the voice of God declaring that the translation was correct. Oliver Cowdery, the first signer, went on missions and did much good, but he lost the spirit of the gospel and fell. In 1838 he was cut off the Church. David Whitmer lost his standing at the same time and Martin Harris in the same year. For nine years Oliver Cowdery was separated from the Church, and for thirty-three years Martin Harris remained away, but both were finally rebaptized and died in the Church. David Whitmer never came back, but he and his fellow-witnesses affirmed time after time that they had really seen the angel and beheld the golden plates.

The Prophet was permitted to show the record to eigh other persons as an additional testimony. They were Christian, Jacob and John Whitmer and Peter Whitmer, Jun., Hiram Page, Joseph Smith, Sen., and his sons Hyrum and Samuel H. Smith. These men handled the plates and seriously judged them to be of gold and engraved with ancient work. They were without exception unflinching in their testimony that the Book of Mormon is true.

When John the Baptist visted Joseph and Oliver to give them the Aaronic Priesthood he promised that the Priesthood of Melchizedek would later be conferred upon them. They became very desirous to receive this and made it a matter of prayer. As they were once asking the Lord about it they heard His voice directing them to ordain each other, but not until they were accepted as spiritual teachers by those already baptized. Sometime after this, during the month of June, 1829, Peter James and John appeared to them and conferred upon them the holy Priesthood. These three had been chosen by Jesus Christ when He lived on the earth to preside over the Priesthood and it was their office to restore it when the Lord chose to permit men on the earth again to hold it.

The work of translation was now drawing to an end and a contract was made with Egbert B. Grandin, of Palmyra, to print five thousand copies. In August, 1829, the work of printing began. The copy used was not the original manuscript, but the whole was rewritten and Joseph preserved the original. Three thousand dollars was the price agreed on and Martin Harris gave security for its payment. In March, 1830, the book was issued to the world.

When the work was finished Joseph delivered the sacred treasures to the angel Moroni and left them to be guarded by him. Treasure seekers have searched for them, the stone box has been torn away, but they have been sought in vain and they will remain hidden until the Lord's own due time.

Oliver Cowdery was left by Joseph to watch over the work of printing and the Prophet was free to visit his wife at Harmony. It was, however, a busy winter for him, for he received many revelations concerning the organization of the Church, and he spent much time in declaring the truth to all who would listen.

CHAPTER X.

1830.

THE CHURCH ORGANIZED—JOSEPH ACCEPTED AS LEADER —THE HOLY GHOST CONFERRED—JOSEPH CASTS THE DEVIL FROM NEWEL KNIGHT—THE FIRST CON- FERENCE.

ON the sixth day of April, in the year eighteen hundred and thirty, was organized at the home of Peter Whitmer in Fayette, Seneca County, New York, the Church of Jesus Christ of Latter-day Saints. Six men made the organization, and their names are Joseph Smith, Jr., Oliver Cowdery, Hyrum Smith, Peter Whitmer, Jr., Samuel H. Smith and David Whitmer.

It was a humble beginning for the Church of Jesus Christ, as was His beginning humble when He came upon the earth. At that time mighty mansions and gorgeous palaces stood as the dwelling places of royalty, but the Great King was born where cattle and beasts of burden were housed. Now splendid churches and magnificent cathedrals stood as places of worship, but Christ's Church was organized and the mighty work of salvation begun in a house of logs in an obscure village and by country men of little worldly learning.

But the Spirit of God and the holy Priesthood were there. Jesus had revealed the manner of organization and the day, and had commanded that it be called after Him since it was His Church. The six men had been forgiven of sin through baptism. Under these circumstances the rudeness of the surroundings was of little account.

The meeting opened by prayer. Joseph and Oliver were first accepted as spiritual teachers, and then Joseph laid his hands on Oliver's head and ordained him an Elder in the Church of Jesus Christ of Latter-day Saints. Oliver ordained Joseph to the same office, and they administered the sacrament. They now possessed the authority to confer the Holy Ghost, and they did so by laying their hands upon the heads of their companions, and at the same time they confirmed them members of the Church.

As on the day of Pentecost when the Holy Ghost, coming down from Heaven like cloven tongues of fire, gave to the Apostles new understanding, so now the minds of those who received it were filled with light. Some prophesied, and all rejoiced and praised God with thankful hearts. To Joseph was given a revelation calling him to the leadership and Oliver to the place of second Elder and preacher in the Church, and commanding the members to give Joseph their obedience. The Spirit also directed Joseph and Oliver to call out and ordain some of the members to different offices in the Priesthood.

A number of persons besides six members were present at the meeting on the sixth of April and they soon asked that they might be baptized and received into the Church. Joseph's father and mother and Martin Harris were among these. On the following Sunday, April 11th, Oliver Cowdery preached the first sermon of this dispensation of the Gospel. The meeting was again at Peter Whitmer's house and many were present. Six more desired baptism, and Oliver performed the ordinance in Seneca Lake. A week later he baptized seven others in the same place.

Soon after the Church was organized the Prophet set out to visit the family of Joseph Knight, at Colesville, Broome County. You remember that Mr. Knight had helped Joseph and the work a year before by bringing provisions to Harmony. In gratitude Joseph now carried to him what is better than food in the greatest hunger—the Gospel. He was very kndly received and had the privilege of holding a number of meetings. Many honest souls became interested and sought for testimonies.

Newel Knight, the son of Joseph Knight, was one of these and had promised the Prophet that he would pray in meeting. When the time came, however, he was unwilling, and said that he would pray first in secret. Joseph could not induce him to call upon the Lord there. Newel came back from the woods next morning, where he had retired, very much distressed. He had tried to pray, but he felt he had done wrong to refuse when called upon and now it was very hard to ask the Lord for light. He grew ill and sent his wife for Joseph.

When the Prophet reached the house Newel was in a frightful condition. His features and limbs were twisted out of shape and he was being thrown violently around the room. A number of persons had come, but they knew not what to do. Joseph at length caught his hand and Newel immediately spoke and begged the Prophet to cast the devil out of him. Joseph rebuked the evil spirit, and in the name of Jesus Christ commanded it to depart. Newel was instantly freed from it, and declared that he saw the devil come out of him and disappear.

He was in his natural state only for a moment. Another power seized him and raised him to the ceiling where he remained for a time unconscious. But this was the Spirit of God, not of the devil and when he came to himself he told of a heavenly vision of unspeakable beauty that had been given him.

Those present in the room were astonished. They had seen the destroying power of Satan and the enlightening power of God. They had beheld a miracle such as the world had not seen since the time of the Apostles, and they were convinced that Joseph held the same power as did they of old.

Joseph soon went back to Fayette, and continued his teaching among the people. On the first day of June, 1830, the first conference of the Church was held, at the Whitmer home. It opened by singing and prayer and the sacrament was administered. A number of confirmations were made and the Holy Ghost again descended upon the Saints. The spirit of prophecy rested upon some, while others beheld glorious visions and sank to the floor overcome.

Newel Knight, who had journeyed to Fayette shortly before and been baptized by David Whitmer, had the curtain of heaven again drawn aside. He looked upon his Redeemer Jesus sitting beside the Eternal Father, and he realized that some day it would be his blessed privilege to come into their presence and dwell forever. The future was unfolded before him and he saw the progress of God's Kingdom on earth.

Much instruction was given the Saints, and they were filled with gratitude for what they had seen and heard. Their hearts overflowed with joy and love and they felt eager to press forward in the work. Once more believers came forth and requested baptism, and David Whitmer was appointed by the Prophet to perform it.

CHAPTER XI.
1830.

BAPTISMS AT COLESVILLE—JOSEPH ARRESTED—DAVIDSON
AND REED ON THE DEFENSE—SUFFERING LIKE THE
MASTER—NARROW ESCAPE FROM MOBS.

WHEN the conference of June 1st, 1830, was over Joseph went to his home at Harmony after a somewhat long absence. He had no time however, to settle down and rest; he was still needed in the work of our blessed Master, and so taking his wife with him he set out for Colesville accompanied by Oliver Cowdery, David and John Whitmer.

Many persons were there who had faith in the Lord and in His work and had repented of past wrong doing. They now desired to be cleansed from sin by baptism, and to be given the Holy Ghost that they might be numbered with the Saints.

It was Joseph's intention to have the baptism performed on Sunday, and on Saturday afternoon he had the others placed a dam across a stream near Mr. Knight's house so that the water would be deep enough. The baptizing had to be put off, however, for during the night the dam was torn away by a mob that had been aroused by the ministers of the neighborhood. It would be interesting to know the texts used that Sun-

day by these pastors who were hired to lead their
flocks in Godly and peaceful paths.

Monday morning early the dam was again built
before the mob was astir, and Oliver Cowdery baptized
thirteen persons. Among these was Emma Smith, the
Prophet's wife. It was a joyful occasion for Joseph.
Before the baptizing was finished the mob had come
together and begun to show an ugly spirit. Joseph and
his friends retired to Mr. Knight's house. The mob
followed and tried to pick a quarrel, but the brethren
would not quarrel and so these bad men had no excuse
to hurt them although they would have liked to do it.

A meeting was set for the evening, to confirm
those baptized. The people had gathered and were
just ready to commence when in walked a constable and
arrested Joseph on the charge of being a disorderly person, and setting the country in an uproar by preaching the Book of Mormon. What a charge! Joseph
had held a few quiet meetings in private houses, and
the uproar was not begun by him.

You can imagine that the people were surprised
and some, no doubt, were pretty angry, but Joseph allowed himself to be arrested quietly. He acted so like a
true gentleman—he always was a gentleman—and had
such an honest face and manly bearing that the officer
made up his mind that he was no rascal but a true man,
and straightway became his friend. And it was fortunate for Joseph that he did, because he had intended
to lead the Prophet into a trap. Of course, now he
changed his mind and told him that the arrest was
only a trick to get him away from his friends and let
him fall into the hands of the mob, which was lying in
wait for him on the road. The constable determined
to try a trick of his own on the mob, and they set out
together in a light wagon.

They had not gone very far before they came upon a crowd of evil-looking men, who gathered about to seize Joseph as soon as the wagon stopped. The constable drove in among them and they awaited his signal. Suddenly he seized his whip and gave his horse a cut and before the ruffians could stir the wagon was just out of their reach. Then began a great race—horse against man, and the horse was getting the best of it. The mob, though they ran as fast as they could, were being left behind, and Joseph and the officer were breathing more easily, when suddenly off came the wagon-wheel. What a plight they were in! If they had stopped to say bad words about their luck they would probably have been caught, for the mob were racing down the road like mad, but they did not swear, they jumped from the wagon, replaced the wheel, fastened it, and away they sped again just in time to escape.

They continued to South Bainbridge in the adjoining county and here secured a room in a tavern for the night. The constable gave Joseph the bed while he slept with his feet aaginst the door with a loaded musket at his side. They were not disturbed.

Next day the Prophet came as prisoner into court. It was the first time that he had ever been tried on any charge. Many times afterwards he was taken before courts for trial, and yet in no case was he ever found guilty. But though he suffered so much from wicked persecutors he never refused to submit himself to the law.

When the constable had come and taken Joseph away from the meeting, it broke up, and Joseph Knight went to two of his neighbors, James Davidson and John Reid to engage them to defend the Prophet in court. These men were honorable, intelligent farmers who understood well the principles of justice and the laws of the land. Though they had never seen Joseph and were in no way connected with the Church, they consented to take his case in spite of the violent prejudice against him.

Mr. Reid afterwards said that when asked he was at first unwilling on account of other work, but before he could refuse he heard a low voice say, "You must go to deliver the Lord's anointed!" The messenger had not spoken and had not heard the voice, and Mr. Reid felt that he had received instruction from heaven. He willingly took the case, feeling sure of success.

The prosecution was carried on by a Presbyterian named Seymour, and he tried by false witnesses to win the case, but Joseph's lawers pleaded well, and the judge set him free. He was immediately arrested again by another constable and taken back to Colesville, Broome County, to be tried there. They stayed over night at a tavern, and during the evening, the officer invited bad men in to join him in abusing the Prophet.

What they did there would have shocked a decent heathen. Joseph was a helpless prisoner in the hands of an officer of the law and there was no reason for thinking him guilty of any crime. Yet that coward officer with his associates spit upon him, and cursed him, and then pointing their fingers at him told him to prophesy. You all have heard how Judas led the multitude against Jesus as He prayed on the Mount of Olives, and how they took Him to the house of Caiaphas the high priest to bring false witness against Him. And there they buffeted Him, and spit upon Him, and told Him to prophesy. Joseph thought of this, and though his sensitive nature must have sickened at the treatment, yet he remembered that he was only servant and that the Master had suffered thus. In both cases it was the same low, cowardly spirit of Satan, the spirit that always seeks to pollute the pure and unprotected.

The Prophet had eaten nothing since morning and was hungry and tired. He asked for food, and the constable gave him a few crusts of bread. He then offered security for his appearance and asked that he might be allowed to spend the night at home. This was refused. He was compelled to sleep against the wall and the constable took away all chance of comfort by lying at his side and holding him all night long.

Next day Joseph was again tried, and the same lawyers and witnesses were present to prosecute him, as on the day before. He was glad to find there also the men who had so ably defended him. The evidence against the Prophet was shown either to be false or to have no bearing on the subject. Lawyer Seymour sought to prejudice the court by a violent speech, but Mr. Davidson and Mr. Reid spoke with such astonishing power in his behalf that the accusers cowered before them. They each thanked God that they were permitted to defend a man whose character was so free from guilt.

So effective was the defense of this case that many who had wished the Prophet harm now became his friends. Even the constable who had been so unmanly, asked his pardon and offered him aid. The officer told him that the mob had gathered and was determined to tar and feather Joseph and ride him on a rail, since he could not be injured legally. He led the Prophet out by a secret way and Joseph escaped. Next day with his wife he returned to his home in Harmony.

Those baptized at Colesville had not yet been confirmed members of the Church, because such a bad, un-American spirit had taken hold of the people there that Joseph and his friends hardly dared to be found in the neighborhood for fear of being hurt or killed. After a little while, however, he and Oliver came on foot from Harmony, but they had no sooner reached Mr. Knight's house than their enemies, learning they were there, formed a mob and came to capture them. Now what should the two men have done in such a position? They might have remained, determined to have their rights, and with the help of their friends fought the mob. They were not afraid, Oliver was brave, and Joseph Smith did not know what fear was. But they were ministers of peace, and peace could be had only by going away, and they went. They did not stop for food or drink, but hurried to escape, for their enemies were following like a pack of bloodhounds. Several times they were nearly caught, but they were strong men and outran their pursuers. They traveled all night and reached home in the morning, pretty thoroughly tired out.

In July, 1830, Oliver Cowdery left Joseph and went to Fayette to labor there. In his place, as scribe to the Prophet, came John Whitmer, and Joseph with his help began to re-write and arrange the revelations that he had received up to this time. Many had been given, and it was necessary that they be kept for the use of the Church in the future.

CHAPTER XII.

1830

FIGHTING THE EVIL ONE—THE MOB BLINDED—PRESI-
DENT ALONE TO RECEIVE REVELATION FOR THE
CHURCH—FIRST MISSIONARY MOVEMENT—WORK-
ING IN THE WEST.

WHEN Joseph first visited the hill Cumorah the
Lord let him look upon the kingdom of heaven
and upon the kingdom of hell. He saw the powers of
each, and the methods and influences that each used.
This vision was of great value to him throughout life.
The contrast made him desire with all his heart to
reach heaven and kept him on the alert at all times to
escape hell. What was also very important, it gave
him a complete knowledge of the practices and weapons
of Satan, the enemy of truth.

All this he beheld in vision, but through the following years in real life he saw these powers of evil at
work, and he had to fight against them. Thanks to
the knowledge given him, to his faithfulness and to the
help of the Lord, he came off victor in every engage-
ment. He had met Satan in the thieves and murderers
that tried to steal the plates, in the lying ministers that
sought to blacken his character, in the violent devil that
nearly destroyed Newel Knight, and in the mobs that
only recently attempted to capture and kill him.

It was now necessary for him to meet another attack of the evil one, and it gave him more grief than
any up to this time. While working with John Whitmer, at Harmony, probably during the latter part of

4

July, 1830, Joseph received a letter from Oliver, who was at Fayette, commanding him in the name of the Lord to erase part of a revelation he had received.

Joseph saw that Satan was now in the flock and that Oliver had been deceived by him. He wrote asking by what authority Oliver commanded him to change the words that God had spoken. He soon visited Fayette and found that the Whitmer family had joined with Oliver. He reasoned with them and one after another they came to see their error and repented sincerely.

After returning to Harmony the Prophet was visited by Newel Knight and his wife. A little meeting was arranged, and Joseph started to buy wine for the sacrament, but an angel appeared and told him not to use wine for this purpose unless made by themselves. Since that time throughout the Church wine has never been used except when new and home-made. At the meeting Emma and Newel's wife were confirmed, and though only five members were present they had an enjoyable time, for the Spirit of the Lord was there.

Near the end of August, Joseph with his brother Hyrum, David and John Whitmer, went to Colesville to confirm the others whom Oliver had baptized. It was a dangerous thing to do, so they prayed that the eyes of evil men might be blinded and that they might fulfill their purpose. Near Newel's house they met many of their enemies working on the road. They looked closely at the brethren but failed to recognize them.

A good meeting was held that night; the confirmations were attended to and the sacrament was administered. Next morning Joseph and his companions went home. Soon after they left, an angry mob surrounded the house and spent the rest of the day in wicked threats against the Saints.

The spirit of persecution had been growing in Harmony through the diligent efforts of a Methodist minister who would not mind his own business. Through his lies Isaac Hale was at length prejudiced and refused to protect Joseph any longer. Soon after the Prophet returned from Colesville the last time, Newel Knight came with his wagon and moved him to Fayette on the invitation of the Whitmers.

Here was another trial. Hiram Page, brother-in-law of David Whitmer, had been receiving revelations through a peculiar stone. They were directed to the Church, though they were contrary to the Gospel as explained both in the Bible and in the revelations given through Joseph. Oliver Cowdery and the Whitmer family were again deceived.

Joseph was grieved. At Colesville the hearts of strange men were filled with hate, at Harmony his friends and relatives had turned against him, and now at Fayette his brethren were rejecting him and the Lord. He went quietly to work and induced Oliver to pray with him. An answer came in a revelation of very great importance. The Lord told Oliver that Joseph Smith, Jr., was the only man that should receive revelations for the Church, until another should be appointed in his stead. Every faithful man may be directed by the Lord and be taught by the Holy Spirit, but the president alone has the authority to command the Church in the name of the Lord.

A conference was held September 1, 1830, and Joseph, of course, presided. He was very careful and wise and he at length convinced Hiram Page and the others that the revelations were from the devil. They were rejected by all, and again they repented for lack of faith. The Lord forgave them, for His Spirit rested with power upon the conference and brought harmony and love and greater faith. At this time the glorious principle of the gathering was revealed, and that Zion should be built up in the land bordering the Lamanites.

Parley P. Pratt who had recently been baptized in Seneca lake by Oliver Cowdery came again to Fayette after carrying the Gospel to his kindred in eastern New York. He himself had received it in a very strange way. In the beginning of the year 1830, he prayed that he might understand the scriptures. He had always loved them and studied them diligently, but after the Lord in answer to his prayer enlightened his mind, he saw how ignorant the world was of their true meaning. He felt called to preach the truths, and after selling his house in the backwoods of Ohio where he lived, and settling his affairs, he set out with his wife depending entirely on the care of the Lord. In his wanderings he was directed by the Spirit to those who had heard the Gospel and he hastened to Fayette where he was baptized.

About a month after the conference the Lord revealed through Joseph that Parley P. Pratt and Ziba Peterson should go on a mission with Oliver Cowdery and Peter Whitmer, Jr., to preach the Gospel to the Lamanites. This was the first time that men bearing the holy Priesthood went forth to preach the word since the time of the Apostles of Jesus. Tens of thousands have now been bearers of the same glad message.

They set out preaching where they had a chance and distributing Books of Mormon to many honest souls. They visited the Cattaraugus Indians, near Buffalo, New York, and then made their way to Kirtland, Ohio. Here they met Sidney Rigdon, who less than two years before had baptized Elder Pratt into the Reformed Baptist church. They gave him a Book of Mormon. He read it and believed, and immediately sacrificed his profitable employment as minister to join the Church.

Others came forward in great numbers and were baptized. Worthy men among the converts were given the Priesthood, and among these were Sidney Rigdon, Lyman Wight and Frederick G. Williams. The last named went with the brethren on their mission to the West.

After spending two or three weeks at Kirtland they journeyed on, passing through, as they went, many hardships and strange adventures. They preached to the Wyandots, a tribe of Indians living in Ohio, and to many white people, and at length reached Independence, Jackson County, a small town on the western border of Missouri. They passed onto what is now the State of Kansas and preached to the Delaware Indians until expelled by government agents. Then they took up their labors in and about Jackson County, little knowing at the time that here should be the center stake of Zion and the holy city.

CHAPTER XIII.

1830-1831.

THE WESTWARD MOVE BEGINS—KIRTLAND—THE HIGH PRIESTHOOD CONFERRED—JOSEPH GOES TO MISSOURI—ZION DEDICATED.

WHEN the brethren had set out on their mission to the West, Joseph busied himself in his work at Fayette. Men were coming to him from time to time to learn what the Lord desired for them, and through him revelations were given for their benefit. Other subjects were being revealed and among them were matters of great importance to the Church. Joseph also began the revision of the Bible in order that the scripture, unchanged, might be given the Saints.

In December Sidney Rigdon and Edward Partridge came to Fayette from Kirtland to offer their services to the Lord. Edward Partridge had heard the Gospel and believed, but had not been baptized. Joseph, therefore, baptized him and ordained him an Elder. The word of the Lord came unto Joseph calling these two men to labor in the ministry.

The Prophet was directed soon after this to leave off translating and to spend his entire time in ministering to the Church and in preaching. The Saints, who now numbered about seventy, in New York, were to leave that State as soon as practicable and gather to Ohio. It was therefore necessary for him to inspire them with faith for the trials of this move and to give other honest souls a chance to join the Church.

On the 2nd of January, 1831, a conference was held at Fayette, being the third since the Church was organized. It was a glorious time for the assembled Saints, for besides the regular instruction a revelation came from the Lord telling them that He would give them a land of promise and that they should possess it eternally. He promised, too, that He would come at a future day and rule as King.

According to the instruction of the Lord, Joseph set out from Fayette in the latter part of January for Ohio. The Saints were to follow in the spring, and it was necessary to find out the conditions and prepare for them. He was accompanied by his wife and by Sidney Rigdon and Edward Partridge. They all reached Kirtland in safety and immediately after, on February 4th, 1831, according to a revelation, Joseph ordained Edward Partridge to be the first Bishop in the Church.

The Prophet now made his home with Newel K. Whitney and occupied himself in translating the scriptures, receiving revelation, discerning and casting out false spirits and guiding the Church. Since the Prophet obtained so many revelations now, it might be well to describe how one was given.   Parley P. Pratt and others say that it was dictated by Joseph to the person writing, slowly and distinctly, sentence after sentence. When one part was spoken the Prophet paused until it was written.   If written correctly it seemed to vanish from his mind and the next was spoken.   If a mistake was made by the scribe, the Prophet did not go on until it was corrected.   There was no hesitation in going forward, and no changes were made after the revelation was written.

A conference of the Church was held at Kirtland June 6, 1831, and all the Elders and Saints that could be gathered together were present.   The Holy Ghost was made manifest in its workings upon the Prophet and many of the Elders.   The spirit of evil was also shown to be present, but as soon as discerned it was rebuked in the name of the Lord Jesus, and vanished. The High Priesthood, a degree of the Melchizedek higher than the Elder, was conferred for the first time on a number of faithful men.

On the day after the Kirtland conference the Prophet was directed to set apart a number of the Elders for missionary work.   They were to travel westward two by two until they reached Missouri, preaching the Gospel on the way.   It was promised that the next conference of the Church would be held in Missouri, on the land that the Lord had appointed for Zion.   About thirty Elders were called, only two of these being sent eastward.

On the nineteenth day of June, 1831, Joseph **left**

Kirtland for the West in company with Sidney Rigdon, Martin Harris, Edward Partridge, Joseph Coe,
W. W. Phelps, and A. S. Gilbert and wife. They
crossed the State of Ohio by stage and boats and took
steamer from Cincinnati down the Ohio river to Louis-
ville, Kentucky. After a delay of three days they again
sailed down the Ohio to the Mississippi and up that
river to St. Louis. The party divided here; Joseph and
Elders Partridge, Harris, Phelps and Coe crossed Missouri to Independence, Jackson County, by foot, and the
others sailed up the Missouri river.

The meeting between Joseph and Oliver and the
Elders with each was a very happy one. For nine
months they had been separated and now they were
united again, a thousand miles from where they parted.
They saw one another full of faith and zeal for the
progress of the Lord's work, and they wept with joy.

They stood upon the land of Zion, and realized
that it was holy ground, for here the New Jerusalem,
the celestial city, shall be built. They looked upon it,
too, as the immediate gathering place of the Saints and
rejoiced at its goodliness. The land was a prairie of
deep, fertile soil and covered with a fragrant and
many-colored growth of flowers. Along the edges of
the streams, timber in great abundance and variety
grew, and scattered among this was an underbrush and
shrubbery that bore grapes, nuts, crab-apples, persim-
mons and berries of all kinds.

The land was indeed beautiful, and was a fit gathering place for the Saints. By their industry they
would, if unmolested, build up a great civilization there
and make it indeed a Zion. The future seemed very
bright. Joseph and his companions knew that the Lord
had promised the land to His people as an eternal inher-
itance, but fortunately they did not know of the deeds

of violence, the murders and awful crimes to be committed there before the Saints should build the holy city of peace.

August 2, 1831, under Joseph's direction, Sidney Rigdon dedicated the land of Zion by prayer as the gathering place of the Saints, and at the same time twelve men, in honor of the twelve tribes of Israel, carried and set in place a log for the first house to be built there. This was twelve miles west of Independence, about where Kansas City, Missouri, now stands. On the following day Joseph dedicated the spot where the temple is to be built, a little west of Independence. Eight men were present. The fifth conference of the Church was held, as the Lord had promised, in the land of Zion. It was on the 4th of August. The congregation was made up mainly of the Saints who had come from Colesville, New York, led by Newel Knight.

On August 9th, the Prophet and ten Elders set out down the Missouri river in canoes, but on the third day Elder W. W. Phelps, saw Satan in a frightful form riding on the waters, and it was revealed to Joseph that they should not trust themselves on the river but travel on land. In company with Oliver Cowdery and Sidney Rigdon the Prophet reached Kirtland, August 27th, having been absent a little over two months and having traveled two thousand miles, much of the distance on foot.

CHAPTER XIV.

1831-1832.

JOSEPH was now in Ohio, and for a number of years he made his home there. The Saints were in two bodies; one part gathered about Kirtland, a few miles from Lake Erie in the north-eastern corner of Ohio, and the other about Independence on the western border of Missouri. It was a journey of one thousand miles from one stake to the other and yet for about eight years they were separated. Why did they remain apart? Since that time the Saints have kept together. Now when they have grown in strength and numbers, colonies go out and make homes in Mexico and Canada and other places, and yet the headquarters of the Church and most of the Saints are in Utah. Why did not all in Ohio move to Missouri, the land which the Lord had said was Zion? He had good reasons for keeping some of the Saints at Kirtland, and you will understand them if you go on with this work.

Joseph was not rich, and though he could make more when he turned his mind to business, yet the Lord needed his energy and time for work of a good deal more importance. So instead of building himself a home he went to live at the house of John Johnson at Hiram, Portage County, about thirty-five miles south-east of Kirtland. Sidney Rigdon went with him and together they worked on the translation of the Bible, Joseph translating and Sidney writing.

But there were many other things to do besides translate. W. W. Phelps was sent back to Missoui to begin publishing a monthly paper called the *Evening and Morning Star.* Oliver Cowdery went back also taking with him the revelations that Joseph had received, and the Prophet was busy gathering them. Many special conferences were held, many revelations were received, and much of the time was spent in preaching the Gospel.

A special conference was held October 25th of this year, 1831, at Orange, Cuyahoga County. There were present, twelve High Priests, seventeen Elders four Priests, three Teachers, and four Deacons, besides a large congregation, so you see that most of the grades of the Priesthood were represented. It is interesting to know that James A. Garfield, who later became President of the United States, was born at this place about three weeks after the conference was held.

One day during meeting Joseph had a revelation from the Lord. After it was given those present began talking about revelations. It must have seemed an easy thing to some of them for the Prophet to speak out what the Lord was revealing to him, and they thought they could do it as well as he. The Lord saw what was in their hearts and revealed through Joseph that the wisest among them might try to make up a revelation. Wm. E. McLellin considered that he was the wisest, and tried to write a commandment, but he made a dismal failure. He could not imitate the words of Jesus Christ even in the least of His commandments. After that attempt all those who saw it felt sure that Joseph was a true Prophet.

When the Church was organized in 1830 the Lord

did not command that all the officers should be appointed at once. But as the knowledge and needs of the people increased, He revealed the other offices in the Church and Priesthood. Joseph was not immediately made President with two counselors. For a long time there was no quorum of Twelve Apostles or of Seventy. Men had to be proved, before they could be put into such positions. When the proper time came Joseph was directed to fil up the offices until at length the organization was complete.

It was nearly a year, you remember, after the organization of the Church that Edward Partridge was called to be the first Bishop. He went to Missouri and made his home with the Saints there, and Newel K. Whitney was afterwards appointed, on December 4, 1831, to be Bishop at Kirtland. At this time Joseph received a revelation telling what the duties of Bishop are.

For a year and a half the Prophet had not been disturbed by mobs. When he left Colesville the last time he began to enjoy some peace. But Satan could not be idle very long while Joseph Smith was alive and free, and an opportunity soon came to injure the Prophet. Ezra Booth apostatized and began to lie about him and to fight the Church. The truth is that Satan finds his best tools in the apostates. The devil, you know, is one himself—he apostatized in heaven, and he knows well how to use a person who has denied the faith.

This Ezra Booth had been a Methodist priest, but was converted by seeing some one suddenly healed. He was like Simon, the sorcerer, who offered the ancient apostles money for the power to confer the Holy Ghost, He wanted the Priesthood, not that he might bless people but that he might smite them and compel them to believe and thus make a great display. When he found that he must be humble and pure if he obtained power in the Priesthood he left the Church and wrote false letters to make the people hate Joseph.

Others at Hiram apostatized also and became very bitter enemies. They were even filled with the spirit of murder that they might destroy the servants of God— men cannot be worse than that.

Emma Smith had twin babies that she had adopted when they were only nine days old. In the spring of 1832, when they were nearly a year old they caught the measles. On the night of March 25th, Joseph sat up with the sicker child until late and then lay down beside it on the trundle-bed and fell asleep. A scream of "murder!" from Emma waked him. He was in the hands of the mob and they were dragging him through the door. He loosened one foot from their hold and kicked one ruffian in the face and sent him sprawling down the door-step, with blood spurting from his nose. But there were too many for him, and he could not get free. They cursed him and choked him until he fainted.

When he came to, they were away from the house. Sidney Rigdon was lying on the ground, where they had dragged him by the feet over the rough ground. He was lying there as if dead. They held Joseph off the ground so that he could not spring. They knew how strong and active he was. The leaders of the mob were holding a council to decide what to do.

They brought a tar bucket and tried to push the paddle, all covered with tar, into his mouth, but he twisted his head so that they could only smear it over his lips and face. Then they tried to poison him with nitric acid, but the bottle broke against his teeth and the acid ran to the ground. But the most horrible thing was now to come. They rent his clothes from his body and suddenly one fell upon him like a fury and with his nails tore the Prophet's flesh, and taking God's name in vain he said, "That's the way the Holy Ghost falls on folks." Then they covered his body with tar, and fled.

Slowly Joseph made his way home to Father Johnson's house. When Emma saw him she fainted. They gave him a blanket to cover him and he went into the room where friends were waiting with Emma. They spent the rest of the night in cleaning the tar from his wounded body. Next morning was the Sabbath, and he went to meeting. Standing up boldly before some of the very men who had tried to murder him, he preached a powerful sermon, and in the afternoon baptized three persons.

The spirit of the mob did not die out, they continued to threaten and vex the Prophet and those about him. Sidney was out of his head for two or three days on account of being dragged over the frozen ground, but as soon as he was well enough he hurried away with his sick family from Hiram. One of Joseph's twin babies died from catching cold on that dreadful night, and two days after its death, on the 1st of April, Joseph left for Missouri, in company with Sidney Ridgon, Newel K. Whitney, Peter Whitmer and Jesse Gauge. He arranged for Emma to stay at Bishop Whitney's home.

CHAPTER XV.

1832-1833.

THE VISIT TO MISSOURI—JOSEPH POISONED—BRIGHAM AND HEBER C. KIMBALL COME TO KIRTLAND—PROPHECY OF CIVIL WAR—FIRST PRESIDENCY ORGANIZED.

JOSEPH'S visit to Missouri in the spring of 1832 was not alone to escape the mob, although his life was in danger in Ohio. It seemed necessary for him to see and encourage the Saints in Zion and to attend to other matters.

The little party hurried away from Kirtland and the bad men who wished to kill them followed. Thus they went until they reached Cincinnati, when their enemies gave up the chase. On the journey the boat on which the brethren rode caught fire twice, but no one was hurt. Joseph during his life had many adventures.

Two days after reaching Independence, on the twenty-sixth of April, a general council of the Church was held, and Joseph Smith, Jr., was sustained as President of the High Priesthood. The Prophet had been ordained to this position at a conference in Amherst, Ohio, January 25, 1832, and when the Saints in Zion accepted him he stood at the head of the Church as President. You remember that Joseph was accepted as first Elder when the Church was organized, and he had continued to preside over and to lead it. But now the Lord desired to make the organization more complete, and he was called to be President and

Frederick G. Williams to be counselor to him, though Elder Williams was not ordained to this position until a year later.

While the Prophet was at Independence much other business was carried on, and the most important of this was the order to print three thousand copies of the Book of Commandments. This was the first book containing the revelations from the Lord to the Prophet. At a later time these were printed in the Doctrine and Covenants. At the same conference Elders W. W. Phelps, Oliver Cowdery, and John Whitmer were appointed to review and prepare for the press such revelations as should be deemed proper for publication.

After a very pleasant two weeks' visit among the Saints Joseph departed for home. His journey was made most of the way in a stage. The great railroads now running through the states of Missouri, Illinois, Indiana and Ohio were unheard of then. Only the year before, 1831, the first engine and train of cars in America were run over a fifteen-mile track westward from the city of Baltimore in Maryland. So you see that it took many days to go the distance that can be traveled in one day now, and there was certainly far less comfort and perhaps even less safety in traveling by stage than by railroad.

On this particular journey, while passing through the southern part of Indiana, Joseph and his companions had a thrilling adventure and serious accident. The stage horses became frightened and ran away. It was very dangerous to remain inside, for the high coach was likely to be tipped over and wrecked, and they also found it dangerous to get out. Joseph and Bishop Whitney tried it, and Joseph reached the ground safely. Bishop Whitney, however, was not so fortunate. His foot slipped into the swiftly whirling wheel and the bones of his foot and leg were twisted and broken, and then he dropped, limp and bleeding into the road.

Joseph took his friend to an inn at Greenville and for nearly a month cared for him tenderly. At the end of this time the Prophet rose one day from the table, walked to the door and began vomiting frightfully. Blood and poison came up, and so violent was the retching that his jaw was thrown out of place, and the poison acted so powerfully on him that it loosened his hair. With his own hands he replaced his jaw and then hurried to Bishop Whitney's bed. Bishop Whitney laid his hands upon his head and rebuked the evil power that was afflicting him, and instantly he was completely healed.

But what was to be done now? Bishop Whitney had not yet been able to move his broken leg from the bed, and of course the Prophet would not leave him. He walked into a grove near by to think. About him were fresh graves. He had seen them before, but now he knew what they meant. Suddenly the inspiration of the Lord came upon him and he hurried back to the inn.

He told Brother Whitney that if he would agree to set out in the morning, a wagon would take them to the river where a ferry would be waiting to cross. Here a hack would carry them to the landing, where a boat would be just ready to sail. By eleven o'clock they should be going up the river and would at length reach home in safety. Bishop Whitney's faith was strong and he agreed.

They left the inn next morning and all happened just as the Prophet had said, though he had made no arrangements and knew nothing of the times of sailing. Bishop Whitney was very glad that he had been willing to accept the promises of the Lord punctually. If

5

he had waited until evening or the next morning or until his foot was well, there might have been two more new graves in the wood near Porter's inn at Greenville, Indiana.

After Joseph reached Kirtland he busied himself with the translation of the scriptures and the many, many duties that filled his life and made it such a busy one. He was receiving important revelations, writing letters, organizing and teaching a school for the faithful Elders at Kirtland, called the School of the Prophets, preaching the Gospel, and providing for his family. You may well believe he was busy.

In the fall he took a short trip east with Bishop Whitney and visited Albany, New York and Boston. When he returned, Nov. 6, 1832, he found that a baby boy had just come to his home a few hours before. This was the first of his own children that lived, and he named it after himself, Joseph Smith. The Prophet builded great hopes upon his boy, but they have not been realized.

Two days after he reached home, he was working in the woods chopping down trees when two strangers came to him. They were large, noble looking men, and a little older than he. Their names were Brigham Young and Heber C. Kimball. There in the forest these men of God met, with the beautiful leaves of autumn above them, and no kings ever came together under a canopy of cloth of gold that were so great or so good or so important as they.

Brigham and Heber had traveled three hundred miles by team to see Joseph and they were not disappointed. Joseph with his prophetic eye saw that they were mighty spirits, and he knew and said that Brigham would sometime preside over the Church. While they were still together the gift of tongues came upon

Brigham and he spoke. It was the first time Joseph had ever heard the gift, and he was filled with joy. He understood the meaning of what Brigham had spoken, and said it was the language used by Adam and those who lived before God confused the tongues of the builders at the tower of Babel.

Brigham Young and Heber C. Kimball were both born in Vermont, Joseph's native state, in June, 1801, Brigham's birthday being the first of the month and Heber's the fourteenth. Both moved to New York, as did Joseph, and there heard the Gospel. April 14, 1832, Brother Young was baptized, and on the following day Brother Kimball came into the Church. After their visit to Joseph they returned home to arrange their affairs in order to gather with the Saints.

During the winter the Prophet received a number of important revelations. One was given Christmas day, 1832, concerning war. Joseph prophesied that there should be a rebellion beginning in South Carolina, which should lead to a war between the Northern and the Southern States. He said that the Southern States should call on Great Britain, that slaves should rise against their masters and be trained for war, and death and misery should come to many souls.

Just twenty-eight years after this, in December, 1860, South Carolina withdrew from the Union and other states followed. On the twelfth of April, 1861, in South Carolina began the rebellion in awful earnest by the Southern soldiers firing on Fort Sumter. The Southern States did call on Great Britain, and began the war relying on that nation's aid, although they did not receive the help expected. President Lincoln, in a proclamation September 22, 1862, said that all slaves should be free, and many were then trained as soldiers to fight their Southern masters. The war did cause the utmost death and misery—about one million men were slain, and how many millions were left in misery and sorrow! And thus was fulfilled to the letter what God had shown to His servant Joseph, and Joseph had spoken to the world.

Another revelation that you have heard much about was given in February. It is what we call the Word of Wisdom. If the children of men would only obey this Word, how much knowledge and health and happiness and beauty we should have, and how little sorrow and ugliness and crime!

When Joseph was accepted as President of the Church, you remember that Frederick G. Williams was called to be a counselor, and later Sidney Ridgon was also named by the Lord. At a meeting of the School of the Prophets, March 18, 1833, Joseph set these two men apart; Sidney as first counselor and Frederick as second. The presiding quorum of the Church was now complete, and Jesus and a host of angels appeared before the faithful Elders present to show that God was pleased.

CHAPTER XVI.

1833.

TROUBLE BEGINS IN MISSOURI—THE ELDERS PRAY, THE MOB GETS DRUNK—JULY MOB DESTROYS PRINTING OFFICE AND TAR AND FEATHER THE BRETHREN—THE SAINTS PROMISE TO LEAVE—APPEAL TO GOVERNOR.

ALMOST in the center of the United States is Missouri, one of the most fruitful states of the Mississippi valley. It is a beautiful land with its dales and hills and woodland. The great Missouri river flows through it and the mighty Mississippi, passing by its eastern side, carries its grains and other products to the sea.

It has had a wonderful past, but its future will be more wonderful. Father Adam lived in that land with Mother Eve in their innocence, and they lived there after their transgression. In this day God commanded His Saints to gather there soon after the organization of the Church. They obeyed, but were soon robbed and scourged, some killed and the rest driven away. Later, when the Civil War came, more blood was spilled, and the worst form of war was there, because the people were divided and slew one another.

But the future of the state of Missouri is the most interesting to us. If the Latter-day Saints obey the commandments of the Lord He will soon begin to prepare the land of Zion for them, just as He would have prepared the land of promise by sending hornets before Israel, if Israel had been faithful. There in Jackson County the holy city will be set up as the capital of God's kingdom.

On the sixth of April, 1833, the Missuori Saints, thinking of the happy future, came together on the bank of the Big Blue river to celebrate the birthday of the Church. It was just the opening of spring and all about them was beautiful. They were happy, for by hard work they were making themselves prosperous. They owned their homes, and though they were poor, yet the prospects for all were very bright.

God in His wisdom does not permit us always to see what is before us. If those Saints could have looked upon the dark, gloomy years ahead, they would have been sad indeed. Soon after the meeting of the sixth of April a mob of about three hundred men collected in Independence to make a plan to drive away the Saints. They thought it right on such an occasion to drink a good deal of liquor so that their very worst feelings might rule, but they were too generous with themselves. They became drunk and broke up in a general fight. A few of the leading Elders met together when the mob assembled and prayed that they should do nothing to harm the Saints. This prayer, you see, was answered.

No more was done by the mob until July, and then, through the efforts of ministers and those who called themselves religious men, the people were again stirred up. Minister Pixley was one of the most zealous liars among the enemies of the Saints, and it was greatly due to him that they renewed their persecution. On the twentieth of July a massmeeting was held, and among the five hundred men present were some of the prominent officials of the state.

Col. Richard Simpson was chairman and Col. Samuel D. Lucas was one of the secretaries. The meeting resolved that no more "Mormons" should come into Jackson County, that the "Mormons" there should sell their property and move out, that the *Evening and Morning Star* should be published no longer, and that those who would not obey this order should be referred to their brethren who had "the gift of divination and of unknown tongues, to inform them of the lot that awaits them."

The main reasons given for these resolutions were that the Saints were poor, they were growing in numbers, and the mob feared they were what in those days were called abolitionists, that is, those who wished the government to stop men from holding slaves. The Saints were from the East and North. They of course held no slaves and hated the system of slavery. And yet they were moderate. The constitution permitted men to hold slaves and the Saints had no desire or intention to run over the constitution.

In those days the people of the South were very jealous of their right to hold the black men, and looked with great suspicion on the Northerners. This was shown during the persecution of the Saints in Missouri, and as the Prophet Joseph foretold, it grew and grew until it ended in a bloody war.

A committee of twelve was appointed by the meeting to see the leading Elders and report in two hours whether they would accept the terms or not. Truly the mob were expecting much when they demanded that four or five men should agree in about one hour's time that one thousand two hundred souls should be driven from their homes.

Edward Partridge, W. W. Phelps, Sidney Gilbert and others were seen by the committee, but the brethren asked for more time. The committee refused and returned to the meeting. When the mob heard their report it was decided by a vote of all to destroy the printing office and steal the press and type. They went to Elder Phelps' house where the printing was carried on, drove his family into the street, although Sister Phelps was nursing a sick baby, and then tore down the house. They stole press, type and paper and all else they wanted, and destroyed the rest.

These Missouri ruffians doubtless enjoyed this very much, but it did not satisfy them, they wanted a little rougher sport, and their pleasure was the pain and suffering of others. They found Bishop Partridge at his home, dragged him to the court-house, and tarred and feathered him, because he would not deny the faith or leave the country. Elder Charles Allen suffered the same treatment. With the tar was mixed some acid, unslaked lime or lye, and it burned into the flesh. But these brethren were so filled with the love of God that they felt no hate or bitterness toward their enemies.

Lieutenant Governor Lilburn W. Boggs, who was next to the highest officer in the state, saw all this lawlessness and outrage, and when it was done he coolly said to the Saints, "You now know what our Jackson boys can do, and you must leave the country."

Three days later, on July 23rd, the mob met again, armed and carrying a red flag like the band of anarchists that they were. The Saints knew that bloodshed would follow if they did not consent to leave, so they promised that half would go by January 1, 1834, and the other half by the first of the next April, and the committee for the mob said that no more violence should be done them.

Oliver Cowdery was immediately sent to Kirtland as a messenger to Joseph and the Saints there, and sometime later W. W. Phelps and Orson Hyde were sent to Jefferson City to ask Governor Daniel Dunklin for help. They told him of the things you have just read about, and the many other threats and injuries the Saints had suffered. He said that the attorney-general of the state, the man whose duty it is to advise on points of law, was absent, but when he returned the governor promised to write an answer.

About a month after the petition was written, the governor's answer reached the Saints at Independence. He said that no citizens have a right to take the law into their own hands. "Such conduct strikes at the very existence of society and subverts the foundation on which it is based." But he said that he could not persuade himself that any portion of the citizens of Missouri needed force to teach them this. Governor Dunklin should have looked more closely at the written statements of the mob, which Elders Phelps and Hyde enclosed in the petition. The mob's words were: "Intending as we do to rid our society (of the 'Mormons'), peaceably if we can, *forcibly if we must,* we deem it of highest importance to form ourselves into a company for the better and easier accomplishment of our purpose." This same statement was repeated in other words.

The governor advised the Saints to have their enemies arrested and tried by law in the ordinary way. He said that justices of the peace could issue warrants. But the trouble was that they would not. Throughout Governor Dunklin's term of office he filled his letters with patriotic words, but he did not restore the Saints to their homes and rights. He was perhaps sincere in his desire to do right, but he lacked vigor and strength and waited for extraordinary troubles to mend themselves in an ordinary way instead of doing his duty bravely and with determination. At least, Governor Dunklin was not the lawless brute that was Lilburn W. Boggs who became governor after him.

CHAPTER XVII.

1833.

THE MISSOURI SAINTS HIRE LAWYERS AND THE MOB
    FORMS—NIGHT ATTACK ON BIG BLUE BRANCH—
    TWO DAYS OF CRUELTY AND PLUNDER—THE BATTLE
    —SAINTS GIVE UP ARMS.

THE Saints in Jackson County, taking the advice of the governor, prepared to try by the common methods of law to gain their rights, and they relied on his promise to use force if these means failed. They hired four prominent lawyers and paid them one thousand dollars for their work. How glad we are that they did this! They showed that they loved peace and were seeking it by all means in their power. And this is one more testimony against Missouri.

But at the time, this action of the Saints only made matters worse. Lawyers Wood, Reese, Doniphan and Atchison, wrote under date of October 30, 1833, agreeing to work for the Saints, and on the night of the following day, as soon as the news had spread, the mob came together. There was a branch of the Church on the west bank of the Big Blue river and this the mob chose to attack.

It was night, and the little lone settlement off in the wilderness was at peace. Suddenly fifty armed men whose hearts were full of cruelty appeared, and before the Saints could gather to defend themselves it was too late. They broke into the houses, cursing people with awful oaths. The children and their mothers were terrified and ran out into the darkness to hide in the brush with the wild beasts. The fathers could not even go with them, but were caught and whipped and knocked down with clubs. When the bleak morning came they crept back, but their houses were torn down, their homes ruined.

Gray, cheerless November had come. The voices of the wind and storm were loud and boisterous. The signs of winter were fast appearing. At such a season it was pleasant to gather in the evening about the blazing, crackling fire in the great, open hearth and enjoy its cheerfulness. But this was not the lot of the Saints in Zion.

Night after night without ruth or mercy the mob broke into the homes and drove out men and women, the sick and aged, the little children, and sometimes not daring to go into the houses themselves, the cowards threw stones through the windows. So you see when the Saints went to bed they knew not what horrible scene might be before them when they awoke. How earnestly those little children must have prayed for God to keep them safe during their sleep, and when morning came for Him to guard them through the day! Do you think you are as earnest in your prayers?

On the night of November 1st, the mob was very busy. The men were divided into groups of fifteen or twenty who went about breaking into houses and thrusting poles through the windows. Another body of men, who loved to fill their pockets with stolen goods better than hear the screams of frightened children, gathered about Gilbert & Whitney's store. They burst in through three doors and took what they wished, and scattered other goods about the streets.

When a little band of brethren came up to stop the robbery nearly all the mob scampered off like sneak-thieves, though one of them named Richard McCarty was captured. The brethren took him before Justice of the Peace Samuel Weston, but this officer would issue no warrant for his arrest, and so he was set free, although he was caught in the very act of the crime.

On the next day the Saints in Independence left their homes and camped out together on the prairie, taking as many of the things that were left as they could carry. The mob, therefore, went to the settlement on the Big Blue river to continue their work. In one house David Bennett lay sick. If the mob had been made up of the wildest men of the darkest jungle of Africa they could hardly have been more savage. They dragged him from his bed, almost beat him to death, and shot him in the head with a pistol, but the injury was not fatal. One of the mob was wounded that night, perhaps by one of his companions, but it was blamed upon the Saints, of course.

Upon hearing of this the enemy grew very angry. The Saints had been so long-suffering that they were no longer expected to use the right of every human being to defend himself. The mob said openly that Monday would be a bloody day. Many of the leaders were religious men, and were required to be at Sunday service. Perhaps because they did not wish to miss anything, the murder was put off until Monday instead of being carried out at once.

This general slaughter was probably prevented by the determination of the brethren that they would fight, if fight they must. A company of thirty carrying seventeen guns met sixty of the mob who had turned their horses in Whitmer's cornfield and were hunting a little body of brethren who had fled. The mob cursed and opened fire, wounding a number of the Saints. The fire was quickly returned and two of the mob fell dead, and the rest, leaving their horses and dead companions, broke into flight.

Two of the brethren, Andrew Barber and Philo Dibble, were wounded very seriously. Philo Dibble was healed by the blessing of God and he lived to come to Utah with the Saints. He passed away only recently. Brother Barber died next day and he became the first martyr in this dispensation—unless we call the little foster-babe of Joseph's a martyr. It died, you remember, from the effects of mob violence.

How different was Brother Barber's death from that of the two mobocrats! He gave his life in defense of his brethren, and greater love than that no man hath. The others died while trying to murder innocent men. And when the brethren went to them as they lay dead and deserted in their own blood, they were filled with strange feelings, for they remembered what one of these, Hugh Brazeale, had said during his life: "With ten fellows I will wade to my knees in blood, but that I will drive the 'Mormons' from Jackson County."

This battle took place about sunset. Rumors were at once hurried off to all parts of the country with all manner of false reports, such as that the "Mormons" had taken Independence and were joined by the Indians from across the border. The people rose in arms. Some prepared to come in the morning, others gathered in Independence that night.

They ordered the arrest of Sidney Gilbert and others who had caught the thief McCarty the preceding Friday night, charging them with assault. Of course, they knew that this was not justice—it was the easiest method of persecution. While the brethren were being tried, the mob gathered and cursed and made the worst threats, and the prisoners were taken to jail to save their lives. They were fired on but were not hit, and the next morning were all set free.

On this day, Tuesday, the 5th of November, one of the greatest wrongs ever done to a body of citizens in the United States took place. Lieutenant-Governor Boggs organized the mob into state militia and placed them under Colonel Pitcher, one of the bitterest enemies of the Saints. This man called for all the fire arms the Saints owned, and took them away, directly contrary to the second amendment of the constitution of the United States. He ordered the Church to go from the country at once and to give up the men who took part in the battle the day before to be tried for murder.

The Saints, not wishing to resist the authority of the state, and believing that Lieutenant-Governor Boggs was an honorable man instead of the traitor and murderer they found him to be, did not resist. They relied on his false promise that the arms should be taken from their enemies as well. But, of course, this was never intended. The Saints were deceived. They gave up the only thing that kept the mob from falling upon them. But what an example they set! They preferred to suffer wrong rather than do wrong. Their religion was the Gospel of peace. They had the courage of martyrs, the bravery of heroes, and yet throughout all the Missouri persecution they fought only as the last means of saving wives and children and friends.

CHAPTER XVIII.

1833-1834.

NEW STRUGGLE OF OLD WAR—MOB TURNED LOOSE ON SAINTS—THE TERRIBLE DRIVING—APPEALS TO DUNKLIN AND JACKSON—MOB AND SAINTS HOLD CONFERENCE.

LONG, long ago, before we were born, before any man on earth was born, a great and terrible war was fought. This was in Heaven, between God, our Eternal and Heavenly Father, and a disobedient son, who lusted after more power. The army of the Lord was stronger, whipped Lucifer and his angels and cast them down to hell.

Some on the Lord's side were very valiant, brave spirits, others were not so brave; and some, perhaps, followed the Lord merely because He was more powerful and not because of real love for Him. These last.

when placed on earth, are easy tools for Satan, and
wherever God sets up His work, Lucifer uses them in
his efforts to destroy it.

This struggle in Missouri was just a new battle
of the old war, and it seemed as though Satan's tools
were very thick there and were of the worst kind.   In
one sense the evil one was victor.   The Saints were
driven from Jackson County, and then from place to
place until they fled from the state to save their lives.
And yet the Lord's power is far greater than Satan's,
and if He had willed it, the persecution would not have
taken place; but He let it go on because the Saints did
not obey all His laws and prepare themselves to build
up the holy city.

When, according to Col. Pitcher's order, the weapons of the people were given up, the mob—now state
soldiers—acted like a legion of devils.   They rushed in
companies on foot and horseback from place to place,
stealing, pulling down houses, threatening to murder
women and children, and tying men to trees and beating them.   Ministers took an active part, and Rev.
Isaac McCoy with his gun on his shoulder led one band.

Out on the wild prairie scattered all who could
escape, and there they wandered, homeless and torn
from their loved ones.   Darkness came, and through
the crisp air of the November night the stars shone
down upon their misery.   A few halted at dawn on the
bank of the Missouri river and little by little their
numbers grew.   Each day more came to join them at
the ferry, bringing what they could carry from their
ruined homes.

A great part of the Saints crossed the river into
Clay County, some went into VanBuren and Lafayette
Counties and some scattered in other directions.   Jack-
son proved not the only county where unkindness was

known. And almost all the Saints except those in Clay were driven again. The people in Clay did show some Christian feeling and let the Saints remain.

About a week after the terrible attack of the mob militia, before dawn on the morning of November 13th, all the heavens began to glow with splendid light. Stars shot from their places, leaving behind them a radiant train. All the colors of the rainbow were seen. It was like the most magnificent play of the northern lights. The Saints could easily see this glorious sight—few had roofs over their heads to prevent. They rejoiced, for they took it as a sign of God's glory, and it certainly was. Their enemies saw it also, and they, believing like the Saints that the Lord of hosts was showing His power, were terrified.

Just as soon as the leading brethren could cross the river, they sent out a sworn statement of all that the mob had done, to Governor Dunklin. He ordered a special court of inquiry to be held at once. This was done and Col. Pitcher was arrested for court-martial because he had taken the arms from the Saints.

The governor said he would restore the Saints to their homes by force if they wished it, but that he could not keep the soldiers there to protect them. They themselves had no weapons, and of course did not care to go back and be butchered by the mob. They asked to be organized into a militia, but though this was legal it was never done.

They sent petitions to President Andrew Jackson, asking that the United States troops might be stationed in Jackson County to protect them. The soldiers had to be placed along the frontier somewhere, and the Saints thought if placed there, the mob would not dare to do any violence. The president would not interfere, saying he had no authority to act in this case.

On other occasions President Jackson was not so particular about authority when he wanted to carry out his plans. What an exhibition of weakness in our government! The governor of Missouri and the president of the United States both seemed willing to do what the law would permit, and yet over one thousand people were driven from their homes and kept away, although they used all the lawful means to regain them.

It was a terrible winter for the Saints in Missouri. All the comforts they had gathered about them were gone. They not only were without proper shelter from the storms, but even lacked food. And while they were in this condition, across the Missouri river the mobs were tearing down and burning their empty houses and destroying their harvested crops. During one week in the spring of 1834, one hundred and fifty homes were consumed by fire.

In the latter part of February a regular court of inquiry was held in Jackson County, and about a dozen of the brethren were called as witnesses. A company of state soldiers went out with them as a guard. No sooner had they reached Independence, however, than a strong mob gathered and they were hurried back to Clay County without going into court at all. Blood would certainly have been spilled if they had stayed.

The court found Col. Pitcher guilty of calling out the militia to crush an uprising when there was no uprising to crush, and of making the Saints give up their arms when they were at peace. When Governor Dunklin received this report he ordered that the arms be returned. His orders were not regarded, and here is where his weakness was shown—a strong man would have enforced his own proper commands. Instead of being given back, the arms were divided among the mob, and the Saints never did obtain them.

On the day following the entrance into Missouri of
Zion's Camp, of which you are later to hear much, on
the 5th of June, 1834, the brethren wrote to Governor
Dunklin telling him that the Saints were ready to be
taken back to their homes in Jackson County. You
remember that he had promised to protect them until
they were again settled, but no longer. They had now
obtained new arms, Zion's Camp was coming to help
them, and they believed they could now protect themselves if the mob should rise again to hurt them.

In answering, the governor said that a clearer
right did not exist than that of the "Mormon" people,
who were exiled from their homes in Jackson County,
to return and live on their lands. But instead of rais-
ing troops to go back with the Saints, he tried to persuade them to come to some terms with their enemies.

Through the efforts of him and other prominent
men a meeting was held on the 16th of June in Clay
County between members of the mob and members of
the Church. Different proposals were made but none
were accepted. The mob offered to buy the lands of
the Saints if they would promise that no "Mormons"
should ever come back, but God had commanded them
to build Zion there, and they could not promise that.
The Saints offered to buy the lands of all those who
did not wish to live in the same county with them, but
this did not suit the mob. The meeting grew very ex-
citing and ended by one of the mob stabbing another.

It was an important gathering, for though no
agreement was reached it showed the governor his plain
duty. But excitement and mystery were in the air.
Zion's Camp was near and the people did not know
what to expect.

CHAPTER XIX.

1833-1834.

DURING the year of trouble in Missouri, the Prophet Joseph Smith was not idle. He could not be with the western Saints to share their suffering, but he sent them many letters bearing counsel and the word of the Lord when it came to him. He did not stay away on account of fear. Once when he heard of the terrible cruelties of the mob his generous heart was so moved that he wept aloud, "O, my brethren, my brethren, would that I had been with you to share your fate. Almighty God, what shall we do in such a trial as this!" Much evil is spoken of Joseph Smith, but even his enemies say he was brave.

On the 23rd of July, 1833, the very day, you remember, that the mob, carrying a red flag, gathered in Independence to make the Saints promise to leave the country, the foundation stones of the Lord's house were laid at Kirtland. In a former chapter you were told that the Lord had a good reason for having part of the Church at Kirtland and part in Missouri. You probably begin now to see what it is.

In the autumn of 1833 Joseph went on a missionary journey to New York and Canada in company with Sidney Rigdon and Freeman Nickerson. They left Kirtland October 5th and were gone just a month. Almost every day they had a chance to preach and sometimes to baptize. Their work was very successful, for they not only gained souls at the time but prepared the ground for a future harvest.

One night way up there in Canada they held a meeting in the village of Colburn. The snow fell heavily, but in spite of this the people came together. It was a humble room lighted by flickering candles. Joseph and Sidney tried to tell the people the message of life eternal, but one man was there who made up his mind that they should fail. He was a Wesleyan Methodist. When the meeting had begun he became very noisy. He talked in a loud voice, but there was no sense in what he said. Joseph and Sidney replied to him in an earnest, quiet way, speaking words of truth and wisdom instead of falsehood as he had done, and of course they overcame him.

At Mount Pleasant sixteen persons were baptized in two days, and the signs promised by Jesus did follow the believers. The Holy Ghost rested upon them, and under its influence one sister spoke in tongues. The Saints were all glad when they saw that this was the same dear old Gospel that our Savior preached.

When the Prophet returned to Kirtland he sent many messages to the brethren and sisters in Missouri, but he himself was kept in Ohio, and it was a very busy winter for him. In December Oliver Cowdery and Bishop Whitney brought to Kirtland a new printing press, for although the Saints could not publish the *Evening and Morning Star* in Jackson County, they did not intend to stop printing entirely. The new press was set up. It was decided to publish the *Star* again, and Oliver Cowdery was made editor. The office was dedicated, December 18th.

On the 17th of February, 1834, the first High

Council of the Church was formed at Kirtland. This was made up of twelve High Priests, and Joseph and his two counselors presided over it. The purpose of such a body was to try those who commit sin, for their standing in the Church, and also that the Saints would have no need of going to law when any difficulty arose among them. These men holding the Priesthood were called to hear and discuss all cases, and then the president made his decision. If a mistake was found in this, it could be changed. In ordinary trials two members were appointed, one to speak on each side. If the case was more difficult two were to speak on each side, and if very important, three, but no more than three could ever speak on a side.

Since that time many High Councils have been formed, and now, as you all know, every stake in Zion has one. The President of the Church can no longer preside because he has too many other duties, but the president of each stake holds the position in the council of his stake. These are very important because there are no money charges, and poor men can have justice, as all men can, for the judgments are given according to the laws of God.

Soon after this work was done Joseph began to seek volunteers for a journey to Missouri. The Lord had commanded him in a revelation to gather the young men and the middle-aged and to receive donations of money from the Saints. He promised that if faith and purity were shown by His people He would redeem Zion, and the money was taken that new purchases of land might be made, and those in distress aided.

Joseph started in on this work February 26, 1834. He and Parley P. Pratt traveled eastward from place to place, preaching and telling the Saints that the Lord wished volunteers and money. They were successful in many places. Sidney Rigdon and others went out also. They returned after a month's work.

Soon after they reached Kirtland, Joseph was called into court as a witness against Doctor P. Hurlburt, an apostate, who had been threatening to kill him. Of course it was a very unpleasant thing for the Prophet and still there was nothing else to do. This man was found guilty of threatening to murder, and on the 9th of April he was put under two-hundred dollar bonds to keep the peace, and fined three hundred dollars—to pay the costs of the court.

During the rest of this month Joseph was holding meetings and preparing for Zion's Camp, as the men, who went to Missouri at this time, are called. On the 1st of May over twenty men, with four baggage wagons, were ready to leave Kirtland. They set out and traveled about fifty miles, to New Portage, where they waited until the others came up.

President Wilford Woodruff was in this first party. He had been baptized on the last day of the year 1833, at Richland, New York, and on April 25th he came to Kirtland as a volunteer. Some of you readers have probably heard him tell of his meeting Joseph and how he lent the Prophet his sword to carry to Missouri as the leader of Zion's Camp. President Woodruff served faithfully in this mission as he did on every other during his life, and the friendship that began then between him and Joseph will last throughout eternity.

Two days after the first party left Kirtland, Joseph followed with the main body of the Camp. When the two joined they numbered over one hundred and fifty men. Joseph at once began to organize his little band. Companies of twelve were formed, and each chose its own captain, who gave the men under him their special duties. General officers were also appointed.

The twenty wagons taken by the Camp were heavily loaded with provisions and such things as the poor Saints in Missouri needed.   No room was left for the men; they had to walk along at the side.   They had their guns, pistols and other weapons, but these were only for self-defense.   This was a body of the Priesthood, called by God to go out, not for conquest or plunder, but to protect and minister comfort to those in great need.

CHAPTER XX.

1834.

ZION'S CAMP ON THE WAY—MIRACLE OF BRINGING FORTH WATER—ZELPH, THE WHITE LAMANITE—REBELLION IN THE CAMP—STOP FOR THE NIGHT ON FISHING RIVER—CAMPBELL'S THREAT—THE MOB AROUSED.

ON the evening of the 8th of May, 1834, Zion's Camp slowly made its way into a beautiful grove at the end of its first day's journey.   Each captain chose a camping spot for his company, the firemen builded up crackling fires, the cooks began to prepare food, the horsemen unhitched the horses and tended them, the watermen brought pure water from the brook, the tent-makers pitched the tents and the runners went on errands or carried messages.   You see that each man had his own work and all was orderly.

After supper was over and darkness had come, the Camp gathered about the fires—for the spring air was chilly—and talked of the great work before them.   They may have looked up at the glorious stars and thought of the splendor and the power of the One who made these great bodies and set them in their place, and rejoiced that they were giving up much to do His work.

Suddenly a trumpet sounded, the hour of prayer and sleep had come. In a moment each man was on his knees thanking God for the blessings of the day, asking Him for the blessings of the night, praying Him for the suffering Saints of Zion, for His work everywhere, and for the loved ones at home. Then they lay down to rest and the Camp of Zion was still.

When the spring morning dawned, before the sun rose over the Ohio hills, the men were again astir, each busy at his own work. Again the trumpet sounded and again each kneeled and offered prayer. Breakfast was prepared and eaten, the horses were hitched to the wagons and at a given signal the Camp moved forward on its way.

And thus they went, filled for the most part with zeal and brotherly love, and willing to endure all things. Sometimes they walked in the heat of the day until their feet bled. Often their enemies were thick about them, and guards had to be set at night to keep the Camp from those who would fall upon it in the darkness. But angels traveled with them, as the Lord had promised, and they saw them. Their enemies were often frightened and at one place counted five hundred, although at the time the Camp numbered less than two hundred men.

The blessings of the Lord were shown in many other ways. Once, at the end of a hot June day, they pitched their tents on a broad, treeless prairie, over which they had traveled all day long. They were very thirsty, for the plain had no water upon it and the supply they carried had been gone since morning. When Joseph saw the suffering about him he called for a spade, and picking out a place which all could easily reach, he dug a shallow well.   Water at once flowed into it and the two hundred men and fifty or more horses and mules drank from it. Plenty of water was in the well as long as the Camp stayed there.

Perhaps you have read about the children of Israel thirsting in the wilderness and grumbling sorely at Moses.   At the Lord's command he struck a rock with his rod and water poured forth and all Israel drank of it. But Moses committed sin here, for he spoke as if he and Aaron had done this, instead of giving God the glory.

This miracle was more showy than the one in Zion's Camp but it was in one sense no greater.   The brethren were not complaining and they did not need to be startled by some sudden sign.   But the Lord made the water flow in both cases to give His children drink, and I believe the men of Zion's Camp were more truly thankful than were the Israelites.

Just before the Camp passed from Illinois across the Mississippi river into Missouri, Joseph with Brigham Young and others went up on one of the mounds in the neighborhood to obtain a view of the great river, called the Father of Waters. Here they found an altar built according to the ancient style, and from its foot they dug up the skeleton of a man.   They were surprised to find an arrow-head between the ribs. It was revealed to the Prophet that this was the remains of Zelph, a white Lamanite and a mighty man of God, who had fought as a chieftain under the Prophet Omandagus.   He was killed in battle during the last great struggle of the Lamanites and Nephites.   Of course we know it was not in the last battle of the struggle, because that was fought around the Hill Cumorah. What a glorious gift is the inspiration of God!

It was not until the Camp had crossed the Mississippi that any trouble arose. Of course enemies had often been near, rivers were often deep, roads were often long and rough, but these were all from without —God would protect and care for His servants in such conditions and they could not, therefore, be called troubles. But now real trouble came; it was sin within the Camp, and God would not protect them from that. Only their union and faith had secured their safety in the past. Sylvester Smith openly rebelled against Joseph and the order of the Camp, and others joined with him. The Prophet warned them that the Lord would punish with a heavy scourge, and He did.

As soon as they reached Missouri, Hyrum Smith and Lyman Wight came with volunteers to join them, and the Camp now numbered two hundred and five men, with twenty-five heavily laden wagons. For a few days they remained at Salt river to rest, and here Lyman Wight was made their general. Twenty men were also picked out, with Hyrum as captain, to be a body-guard to the Prophet, for they were now in a country where different men had sworn they would murder him.

After this little rest the Camp traveled on until July 18th, when they stopped for the night one mile from Richmond, Ray County. They expected here to meet an army of their enemies, as the mob had threatened to lie in wait for them at this place. But at daylight the next morning the Camp passed quietly through the town before the people were awake.

They had not gone far on the prairie before a wagon broke down. They stopped and repaired it, but had hardly started again when a wheel ran off another wagon. And so it went all day long. At night, instead of being over in Clay County, as they had hoped

to be, they were only on the Fishing river in Ray.
This was a small stream flowing into the Missouri and
at this point was divided into seven branches. Between two of these, on a high piece of ground, they
halted and prepared to spend the night.

Soon after they stopped, five armed men rode up
and said, with many an oath, that the Camp should see
hell before morning. Sixty men, they said, were coming from Richmond and seventy from Clay County,
and they had sworn utterly to destroy the Camp. With
this warning they rode away. The afternoon had been
very fair, but as night came on black clouds rose from
the west and covered the whole sky.

You ought now to know what was going on outside of Zion's Camp. No doubt you remember the
meeting between the Jackson County Saints and the
Jackson County mob that was held in Clay County,
June 16, 1834. Governor Dunklin and other men
wished the Saints to give way and sell their land, but
this they would not do, and the meeting was broken up
by a stabbing affair in the mob.

James Campbell and Samuel C. Owens, with ten
other angry men, left the meeting, jumped into a boat
and began to row across the Missouri. They wished
to reach Jackson County in order to raise an army to
lead out against Zion's Camp. James Campbell, while
strapping on his pistols before starting, said, with a
bold swagger, "The eagles and turkey buzzards shall
eat my flesh if I do not fix Joe Smith and his army so
that their skins will not hold shucks, before two days
are passed."

How little this man thought of his fate when he
spoke these terrible words! That night the angel of
death overturned the boat in the middle of the river.
James Campbell and six others were drowned and the

rest barely escaped with their lives.   Samuel Owens
floated four miles down stream and landed on an island.
Early in the morning he stripped off his clothes and
swam to the Jackson shore where he borrowed a gar-
ment to cover his nakedness, and, as Joseph says,
"slipped home rather shy of the vengeance of God."
James Campbell's skeleton was found on a pile of
drift-wood in the river, three weeks later, and the birds
of prey had in reality torn off and eaten his flesh.

But there were plenty of men left in Jackson County to call the mob to arms.   This misfortune was no
lesson to them.   They rode over the county telling the
men that the "Mormon" army had come and they
would have to turn out to meet it.   This was a welcome
message, for these were the wild, lawless spirits always
found on the frontier.   They were used to spilling
blood, and they thought themselves very bold and brave.
And so they gathered at the appointed time on the bank
of the Missouri. armed with dirks and pistols and guns,
hoping to kill Joseph Smith and his followers and secure the plunder.

CHAPTER XXI.

THE TERRIBLE TEMPEST ON FISHING RIVER—VISIT OF
COL. SCONCE—CHOLERA IN CAMP—JOSEPH SMITTEN
—SIDNEY GILBERT'S DEATH—PROPHET VISITS ZION.

SHORTLY before sunset on the 19th of June, 1834,
two hundred armed men stood on the southern
bank of the Missouri river ready to cross.   Seventy
armed men waited for them on the opposite shore, and
sixty more, also armed, were marching from Richmond,

Ray County, to meet them. Many of these were ruffians of the worst stripe; they had tied up innocent men and whipped them almost to death, they had frightened women and children out into the darkness and cold, and torn down or burned their houses. Some of them were murderers and all now had murder in their hearts.

A few miles away was another band of two hundred men, just at this time pitching their tents and preparing to spend the night. These had some weapons, also, but were not so heavily armed as were the others. What they had, however, were near at hand and ready for use, for an attack was expected at any moment.

This was a body of God-fearing men, who had come from afar, bringing food to the hungry and clothing to those in need. They hoped also to help their brethren and sisters home to their lands in Jackson County. These men held the Priesthood of the Lord of hosts; they had come at His command; they would not have harmed an animal purposely, and certainly not a human being; but they were determined not to be robbed and killed, and they were ready to fight to the death in self-defense.

If God in His wisdom had seen fit to let the mob come on, blood would have flowed like water, and martyr and murderer would have died together. But He had another fate for His servants than to die there at the hands of blood-thirsty Missourians. This was the hour to show His power. He spoke to the winds and they went rushing over the whole heaven, bearing the black clouds that gathered at His call. He commanded the lightning and the rain and the hail, and they obeyed.

Within a few miles of the Camp of Zion on every side, the hurricane raged. The great hail-storm beat down fields of corn and cut off branches from the trees, and the wind in many places twisted the trunks to splinters. Lightning flashed through the heaven all night long in great zigzag streaks, thunder crashed, and the earth shook.

The puny, weak creatures who had a few hours before defied God's work lost all their boldness and quailed at the sight of His anger. The rain wet them to the skin and spoiled their ammunition. The hail cut holes through their clothing and bruised their bodies. All who could, ran to their homes or hunted nearer shelter. Forty of the two hundred from Jackson County had crossed the Missouri and the boat had gone back for more when the storm came up. Of course the forty were very anxious to go back home then, but they could not swim the great river, and so spent the night with the storm beating down upon them, thinking over their own bad lives.

In Zion's Camp no hail fell, and there was little wind and rain. A few tents were blown down and some of the brethren were wet. Many found shelter in an old meetinghouse, and Joseph sent them to pay for the use of this on the following day. The storm did not frighten the brethren. They knew the Lord had raised it, not to harm them but to keep them from harm. When morning came they found great streams of water flowing between them and their enemies. Big Fishing river which was only ankle deep the night before was now forty feet in depth, and men from the mob said that Little Fishing river rose thirty feet in thirty minutes.

That day the Camp moved about five miles to a place where it would be harder to attack them, and stayed three days. While there, Colonel Sconce with two other men rode up. They came into the Camp, and when they were face to face with Joseph and the brethren the officer trembled so much that he could not stand up. After his nervousness had somewhat passed away he rose and asked what the Camp intended to do. He said he had led armed men from Ray County to fall upon the Camp, but the storm had driven him back, and he knew that an Almighty Power was protecting this people.

The Prophet answered him. He said that the Camp had come one thousand miles to bring supplies to their friends and to help them back to their homes. They hated bloodshed and their firearms were brought only to defend themselves. They intended to obey all laws and harm nobody. He told the sad story of the pitiful sufferings of the Jackson County Saints, and when he ended Colonel Sconce and his friends were in tears. These men were like Paul, the Apostle; they had tried to destroy the truth, believing it was evil. As soon as they learned that they had done wrong they sought to undo it. They rode over the country and told the people the truth about Joseph Smith and his followers.

Cornelius Gillium, sheriff of Clay County, also visited them, and after learning why they had come he told them about the people and the country and advised them how to avoid trouble. After leaving, Mr. Gillium published a true report of what he had learned.

Again on the twenty-third of June the Camp moved, now going toward Liberty, Clay County. Before they reached the town General Atchison, who, as you know, was employed by the Jackson Saints as lawyer, met them. He with other leading men came out to urge Joseph not to pass through Liberty, as they feared trouble. Of course it would have been silly after this warning to run chances of rousing a mob, so the Camp turned, passed by Liberty, and pitched their tents that night at the end of their journey, on Rush creek, among the Saints.

You remember that when Sylvester Smith and others rebelled against the Prophet, about three weeks before this, Joseph told them the Lord would scourge the Camp. And now the scourge came in the form of cholera. Two or three cases had appeared as a kind of warning before the Camp reached Rush creek, and Joseph foretold what would come. He said he was sorry, but he could not help it.

On the following day, June 24th, the terrible disease broke out in earnest and continued four days. There were about sixty-eight cases, and thirteen persons died. Elder John S. Carter tried to rebuke the disease, but it at once seized him and he died. Joseph laid on hands and commanded it to depart from one of those afflicted. The disease did leave but came upon the Prophet. At the same time Hyrum was struck down.

Three times they kneeled and prayed for their lives, and the last time they made up their minds to keep on until they were healed. While they were pleading with the Lord, Hyrum saw in vision their mother back in Kirtland praying for her absent boys. God listened to her prayer and theirs, and they rose up well and strong again.

The Prophet learned a great lesson at this time. He knew that the Lord was going to punish the Camp in this way and he should not have tried to interfere with the Lord's purposes by using his Priesthood to hinder them.

Among those who died was Algernon Sidney Gilbert, who had charge of the Lord's store-house. He was an able, useful man, and had shown much bravery

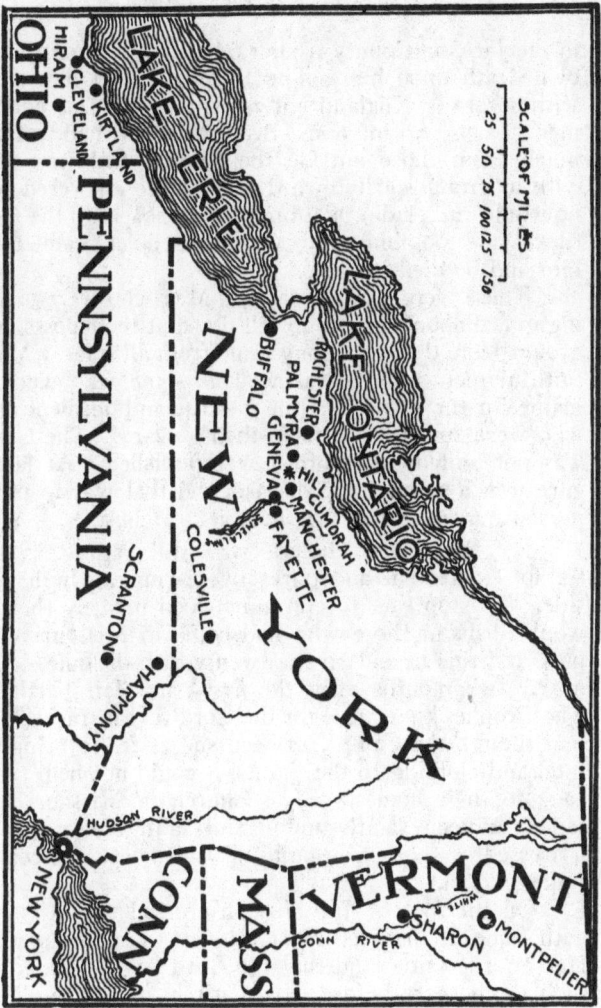

SCALE OF MILES
25 50 75 100 125 150

OHIO
HIRAM
CLEVELAND
KIRTLAND

LAKE ERIE

PENNSYLVANIA

NEW YORK

LAKE ONTARIO

ROCHESTER
PALMYRA
BUFFALO
HILL CUMORAH
GENEVA
MANCHESTER
FAYETTE
COLESVILLE
SCRANTON
HARMONY

HUDSON RIVER

NEW YORK

CONN

MASS

VERMONT
SHARON
MONTPELIER
CONN RIVER

in the Jackson County troubles, but now he brought his own death upon him. The Prophet called him to go with others to Kirtland and after receiving his endowments to go on a mission. Brother Gilbert had suffered much from those outside the Church and was filled with a wrong spirit toward them. He answered that he would rather die than preach the Gospel to the Gentiles. God took him at his word, the cholera came upon him and he died.

These were terrible days. Men who were standing guard about the Camp fell down at their posts, and groans from those in agony came from all sides. Many faithful men suffered, as well as some who were to blame for the scourge. But the true and obedient ones who were smitten will have their reward. The Camp was not united, therefore it was punished. At last a cure was found for the disease, and that was to put a person into cold water or pour it over him.

But while the cholera was still raging in the Camp, excitement and unrest were running high outside. To stop this Joseph announced publicly that he would disband those who had come to Missouri with him, and this he did on the twenty-fifth of June, 1834, nearly two months after the first party left Kirtland. The Prophet knew, too, for the Lord revealed it to him, that though the Camp had been successful in bringing food and clothing to the Saints, it could not help them back to their homes. The Church in Missouri had failed to keep saintly union and faith that must be possessed by those who build up and inherit the center stake of Zion.

On the first of July Joseph crossed the Missouri with some of the brethren and went to Independence. He saw the same land that the Lord had dedicated as Zion three years before, now entirely in the hands of the wicked. It must have made him sad, but he did not lose courage. It was not the part of a fearful man to go into Jackson County as Joseph did. True, he was not known very well in that neighborhood, but if he had been recognized it would probably have meant death

Two days later he organized a High Council in Clay County, for the Saints in Missouri. This was formed like the Council at Kirtland, only David Whitmer and two counselors presided in place of the Presidency of the Church. After visiting another week among the Saints the Prophet set out for home. He reached Kirtland alone about the first of August, after a wearisome journey and after three months of hardest toil and of most valuable experience.

CHAPTER XXII.

1834-36.

A TIME OF PEACE BEGINS—BUILDING THE TEMPLE AT KIRTLAND—THE TWELVE APOSTLES CHOSEN—FIRST QUORUM OF SEVENTY ORGANIZED—JOSEPH TRANSLATES PEARL OF GREAT PRICE—WILLIAM SMITH'S SIN.

MUCH sorrow was felt by the Church because Zion's Camp was not permitted to help the Saints back to Jackson County, and thus redeem Zion—and yet no one was sorry that the brethren had gone to Missouri. It was soon seen that this journey was a trial for certain men before they were called to be Seventies and Twelve Apostles. Perhaps also on account of the will-

ingness of so many and the sufferings they went
through, the Lord blessed the Church for three years
with much peace.

This was a time when mighty things were done.
The Priesthood was more fully organized, the temple
was dedicated, and the Gospel began to spread more
rapidly. Soon after the Prophet Joseph came to Kirtland he sent forth Elders and Priests and he himself
went for a short time to Michigan. With Hyrum and
others he set out by steamer on Lake Erie, and while
on their way they had a laughable experience. One of
the passengers named Elmer told them he knew Joe
Smith very well, and he was glad now that he was dead.
He said Joe Smith was a dark complexioned man, and
he had heard him preach his lies in Bainbridge, New
York, five years before. That man was a pretty bad
liar himself. Joseph was not dead; he was light complexioned; he had not begun preaching five years before, and he had never been in Bainbridge.

During the fall and winter much work was done
on the temple at Kirtland. The people were very poor,
but they did their best, as the Saints have done in Utah
—when they had no money to help on the Lord's work
they gave their labor and their time. Joseph worked
as foreman of the stone quarry, and Hyrum, Brigham,
Heber, and others took up their humble toil with him.

Besides this work, High Council meetings were
held very often, and the School of the Prophets was
begun again. It was a busy time for Joseph, but he
had this motto, and he made it a rule for his future life,
"When the Lord commands, do it." By obeying the
Lord without delay he was able to do much more work
than if he had put things off, just as you boys and girls
can do more work by obeying your fathers and mothers
at once.

One Sabbath afternoon in February, 1835, Brigham and Joseph Young came to the Prophet's house after meeting to sing for him. They had very sweet voices and he loved to hear their hymns. After they had sung, he told them that he had seen the glory of those men who had died of cholera in Zion's Camp and their reward was very great. They talked over the journey to Zion, and Joseph wept. The Spirit of the Lord came upon him and he said that the Twelve Apostles were to be chosen and Brigham should be one of them. He said also to Joseph Young, "The Lord has made you President of the Seventies."

That week the Prophet called a meeting of all who went with Zion's Camp, on the 14th of February. Fifty-six of these men and many other Saints came together. Joseph told them that the time had come when the Twelve Apostles should be chosen, and if the Saints were willing, the three witnesses to the Book of Mormon would pick them out. In one of the early chapters you were told who these men are, but if you have forgotten, look them up and read their testimonies in the forepart of your Book of Mormon.

The Saints voted for them to do it. Each one prayed that God would pour down His Spirit upon them that they might know and do His will. Then they named these twelve men: Thomas B. Marsh, David W. Patten, Brigham Young, Heber C. Kimball, Orson Hyde, William E. McLellin, Parley P. Pratt, Luke Johnson, William Smith, Orson Pratt, John F. Boynton and Lyman E. Johnson. This was not the order at the time, but the Prophet arranged them later according to age, the eldest being first. Now, you know the Apostles stand in the quorum according to the time they were appointed, and the president is the one who has been longest an Apostle.

The Church had been organized nearly five years now, but as you have seen in other matters the Lord was in no hurry to fill up all the offices at once. He in His wisdom chose the time. And yet the calling of the Apostles was no new thought with the Prophet. Even before the Church was organized it was revealed that there should be twelve like the Apostles that were with Jesus.

There was a greater need for the Twelve at this time than there had been before, because now the great missionary movement was beginning, and the work of the Apostles is to direct this. Besides there were now in the Church men who could be trusted with this office, and though six of the first twelve were not faithful, the other half remained true and held their positions when they died and will hold them throughout eternity.

On the last day of this same month of February, forty-five members of Zion's Camp were chosen as the beginning of the first quorum of Seventy. Among these were George A. Smith, Jedediah M. Grant, Joseph Young, and Levi W. Hancock. Brother Smith became later an Apostle, Brother Grant a counselor to President Young, and the other two were presidents of the Seventies quorums throughout the Church.

The Seventies were called to go out and preach the Gospel under the direction of the Twelve Apostles, just as the Seventy in ancient times were sent out by Jesus. When this degree of the Priesthood was begun, the organization of the Church was almost completed, and so when you say that the Church was organized April 6, 1830, remember that it was only partly organized then.

In the early days of May the Apostles started on their missions. They were absent half a year and not only preached but gave much attention to forming conferences. As time passed by they learned their duties and responsibilities. The Prophet Joseph said shortly after their return: "The Twelve are not subject to any other than the First Presidency, and where I am not, there is no First Presidency over the Twelve." This is one of the most important doctrines in the Church; when Joseph died, Sidney Rigdon was not the rightful leader; the Twelve Apostles stood at the head of the Church.

During the summer of 1835 a man came to Kirtland with four mummies and some rolls of Egyptian writing. These had been found in a great tomb way off in Egypt, and it seems almost by accident had been brought to the Prophet, and yet of course the Lord was guiding them. Joseph took the rolls of Egyptian paper and translated the writing better than any of the learned men who had tried before. The owner, Mr. Chandler, gave him a certificate that his translation agreed with theirs but was fuller. Some of the brethren bought the mummies, and Joseph by the aid of the Spirit of God translated the writing and it was later printed in the Pearl of Great Price.

Soon after the Twelve returned from their mission, a very sad thing happened. William Smith, Joseph's brother and one of the Apostles, grew angry at the Prophet over a small matter in a High Council meeting and disturbed the meeting and hurt Joseph's feeling by his unruly conduct. He repented but not very thoroughly, for two weeks later while Joseph was visiting at his house he again grew angry, and struck and injured him. On the 1st of January, 1836, a meeting was held by Joseph, Hyrum, William and their father and uncle. William's feelings were again softened and he asked Joseph's forgiveness and this Joseph gladly gave. The Prophet was always ready to go more than half way to gain peace and good feeling, and if we grow like him and like Jesus we must do the same.

CHAPTER XXIII.

1836.

THE PROPHET'S GROWTH IN KNOWLEDGE—GLORIOUS VIS-
IONS IN THE TEMPLE—DEDICATION—KEYS OF THIS
DISPENSATION CONFERRED—ELDERS GO OUT TO
PREACH.

DO you remember in one of the early chapters of this book it was said that when Joseph began translating the Book of Mormon he could not spell so well as an ordinary schoolboy of these days? His ignorance was not because he was dull or lazy. His energies were spent in the field and forest, and he did not live among people who wrote much or had much knowledge of books. Just as soon, though, as he began spending his time in the Lord's service, his learning grew very fast.

In translating the Book of Mormon Joseph was in the best school a man could attend. The Holy Ghost, which is the spirit of intelligence, inspired his mind and he read and understood a strange language entirely different from our own. When he finished this work he probably had more knowledge of the Egyptian writing than any other man living. The work on the Book of Mormon gave him also a better grasp and understanding of English, and caused within him a thirst for learning that was never quenched. His work in rewriting the Bible helped him very much, and when he translated the books and writings of Abraham and Moses from the Egyptian found on the papyrus with the mummies, he was a well educated man. He understood much concerning the movement of stars and heavenly bodies, and more important, he knew that in the past many of them were worlds like ours and are now as ours will be. He understood how people should be governed. And the highest knowledge of all—he knew our Father in Heaven, better than did any one else on earth.

Think what a blessing this last is! If a bright boy works with an intelligent man whom he admires very much, it is not long until he begins to look at matters just as his older friend does. When that friend is the Lord and the boy is any righteous human being, this same thing happens, only when we look at matters as the Lord looks at them we are not led astray by the opinions of men, but we see the absolute, the whole truth.

The Prophet was now a man thirty years old, and yet with all the other duties he found time to go to school. He studied a number of subjects but was perhaps most interested in Hebrew. A fine Jewish scholar was employed to teach the brethren at Kirtland, and this man said he had never seen a class learn so quickly. The Prophet loved education and true knowledge, and even in the hardest troubles found time to study. He set the example, children, every one of you follow it through life. Study hard and learn all that is true and good and beautiful, and your lives will be far more happy and far more useful.

We have come now to one of the great reasons why God did not direct all of His Saints to go to Missouri but kept a part of them for a number of years in Kirtland. He permitted some to go to Jackson County and buy land there and begin to build up Zion. The Saints were not righteous enough to prevail against the persecutions of their enemies and were driven away from their land. But the feeling was left in their hearts, and in the hearts of their children and in the hearts of all true Latter-day Saints, that we have a claim on Jackson County, and it will be the greatest joy of our lives to go back and redeem Zion, in the Lord's own time.

Now our Father in Heaven in His mercy kept some of the Saints in Kirtland where they could build a temple to Him and receive the holy ordinances and blessings that had been revealed to few people on earth.

It was in July, 1833, that the corner stones of this first temple built in latter days were laid. March 27, 1836, was the day on which it was dedicated, so you see that less than three years were used in building it. The Salt Lake temple was forty years being built, but it is far larger and more costly than was the one at Kirtland.

Before the dedication many glorious things took place that prepared the leading Elders and the Prophet for the great event. One night, in the latter part of January, the First Presidency and some of the Elders from Missouri as well as from Kirtland came together for the purpose of anointing one another. Joseph and his counselors first poured oil on the head of Joseph Smith, Sen., the Patriarch of the Church, and he in turn blessed them.

But the anointings were not the only matters of importance that took place in the unfinished temple that winter night. Angels drew aside the curtains of heaven, and the host that dwelled there and our Redeemer Jesus were seen. The Elders shouted hosannah and glory to God in the highest, and their souls were filled with infinite joy.   The Prophet saw in visions the celestial kingdom of God, and the flaming gates through which the heirs of the kingdom will enter. He saw the glorious throne whereon the Father and Son were seated. He beheld within the beautiful city, Fathers Adam and Abraham, his own parents and his brother Alvin who had died years before.

He was astonished to see his brother there, because he had passed away before the Gospel was restored, but the Lord declared that all who had died without hearing the Gospel, who would have accepted it if they had heard it, will be heirs to the celestial kingdom. Alvin was not enjoying celestial glory at the time of this vision. The Prophet was of course beholding the future, as at this time his parents were both alive, but the doctrine of baptism for the dead had not been revealed, and so the Lord answered him in this way. The explanation is perfectly true. Honest, pure souls who have died without a knowledge of the Gospel are heirs to the kingdom. And yet they can not enter it until baptism has been performed by their relatives or friends here on earth.

The glorious meeting did not end until two o'clock in the morning, and the next night the Elders again met. The Twelve Apostles and presidents of Seventies also met with them and received their anointings and blessings.   Once more angels ministered unto them and mingled their voices in shouts of praise. The gift of tongues came upon the Elders and they had another spiritual feast. A week later High Priests, Seventies and Elders assembled to be blessed and anointed, and like visions and glorious signs were shown unto them.

Early Sunday morning on the twenty-seventh of March, 1836, the Saints of Kirtland with those who had come from Missouri and other places for the occasion made their way to the House of the Lord. They waited patiently until eight o'clock, when the doors were opened and they were received and seated by the Prophet, Oliver Cowdery, and Sidney Rigdon. Less than a thousand could enter, for the building was not very large. At nine, when the presiding authorities were seated on each end of the room, the services began. They sang hymns, prayers were offered, Sidney and others preached and the congregation voted to sustain the authorities. President Joseph Smith offered the prayer of dedication, and this was sealed by the shout from all the Saints who repeated three times, "Hosanna, hosanna, hosanna to God and the Lamb. Amen, amen, amen."

After this there was more speaking, Brigham Young and David Patten addressed the Saints in tongues, and George A. Smith rose and prophesied. Then was heard a rushing like the noise of a mighty wind, and a bright pillar of fire rested on the temple. Angels filled the room and were seen. The whole body of Saints rose to their feet and some spoke in tongues and some prophesied, and some saw glorious visions of eternity. The people of the neighborhood, hearing the rushing sound and seeing the pillar of light, were astonished and ran to the temple to see this strange thing. That night at eleven o'clock the Saints went home, and the dedication of the House of the Lord, the first temple of the latter days was completed.

On March 29th, the Prophet with his counselors and some other Elders met in the holiest place of the temple. There they fasted and prayed and washed each other's feet until morning, when they met with all the officers of the Church holding the Melchizedek Priesthood. The ordinance of the washing of feet was carried out through the whole assembley, the sacrament was administered, and Joseph told the Priesthood their various duties. At nine o'clock in the evening Joseph went home to rest after a most joyful night and day and left the meeting in the hands of the Apostles. During the night the gift of tongues came to some, angels appeared to others, and others, still more blessed, saw the Savior.

On the following Sunday, the third of April, during afternoon meeting in the temple, Joseph and Oliver drew the curtains of the pulpit, thus closing them from the congregation, and kneeled in silent prayer. When they arose they beheld the Lord standing on the breast-work of the pulpit which seemed to be overlaid with pure gold. His hair was white as snow, His face was brighter than the noon-day sun, and His eyes were like flames of fire. He told them that He had accepted the temple, and spoke many blessings on the children of men. His voice was like the rushing of great waters. After this vision ended, Moses came and committed unto them the keys of the gathering of Israel, then Elias gave the dispensation of the Gospel of Abraham; and Elijah, the Prophet, who was carried to heaven in a chariot of fire, conferred the keys of turning the hearts of the fathers to the children and the hearts of the children to the fathers.

These great keys are necessary in this dispensation of the Gospel, for this is to be the fulness of times, when all that has been in the past will be brought back to make the Gospel perfect. Do you wonder why Oliver was with Joseph instead of Sidney Rigdon, or Frederick G. Williams? Oliver had been ordained by Joseph to be an assistant president and so he was at this time of equal rank with them.

During these days of jubilee the Twelve Apostles and worthy Elders received their endowments in the temple and then scattered out into the ever-widening fields of missionary work.   Joseph also went out and spent two months in gathering the blessed harvest.

CHAPTER XXIV.

1836.

THE SAINTS IN CLAY COUNTY—CITIZENS ASK THEM TO LEAVE—CALDWELL COUNTY FORMED—JOHN TAYLOR —LORENZO SNOW—WILLARD RICHARDS.

WHILE the winds of bleak November, in the fall of 1833, were howling through the forest, stripping from the branches the few remaining leaves, twelve hundred robbed and beaten souls made their way from the ashes of their former home down to the banks of the Missouri river.   They crossed, carrying over the things they could save, and placed themselves on the mercy of the people on the other side.   Their landing place was Clay County and the inhabitants proved to be kind—something new for the Saints to meet in western Missouri.

The Clay County people showed considerable sympathy for the strangers during this winter, and permitted them to make their home with them.   For three years the Saints were there, hoping all the time to return to Jackson County and using all lawful means— from trials in a justice's court to an appeal to the President of the United States—to gain their homes and rights.   All efforts seemed to be useless.   Governor Dunklin was as weak as a child, and more trouble seemed to be growing. The Clay County people thought that the Saints could never go back and that if they did not go away somewhere at once, civil war would arise. In those days feeling was very bitter between slave holders and those who did not hold slaves. The Saints were not slave holders, and they were coming into Missouri very fast. The Missourians held slaves and were very jealous of the strangers. Then their religion, though the purest and best in the world, held them from the sympathy of their neighbors. It did look as though war might begin between the Saints and their enemies, for though our people would have made no attack, they would have defended their wives and children to the death.

On the 29th of June, 1836, the citizens of Clay County held a meeting and adopted resolutions asking the Saints to leave. They did it in a gentle manner, saying that they had no right to command the Saints to go, but asked it for the good of all. They suggested that our people move to Wisconsin or some other place where they could be by themselves, but they did not expect them to set out before they had sold their property without loss. They offered to help them find a place, and appointed a committee to raise funds to aid the poor. They also promised to use their influence in causing persecution to cease.

A number of promiment men carried these resolutions to the Saints, and two days later the leading Elders met and acted on them. They agreed to leave, but declared that they were innocent of any lawlessness or crime whatever. They thanked the people of Clay for their kindness in the past and for their offer of help, and in accepting the resolutions asking them to leave, they offered their act as a covenant of peace between the two people forever. What could show more gratitude? Clay County had been kind to them, though no kinder than one Christian should be to another. But the Saints—they were leaving their homes and moving into the barren wilderness to repay that kindness.

Word was at once sent to the Prophet at Kirtland, and he with his counselors wrote letters to the Saints and to the Citizens of Clay. He told our people that they should sell their property at as small a sacrifice as possible, defend their families in case of attack, and stand by the Constitution of our country. The letter to the Clay County citizens was an eloquent defense of the Missouri Saints. It was free from bitterness, though filled with deep sorrow that the innocent people should again find it necessary through the lies of their enemies to become homeless wanderers.

Less than three months after they had consented to leave, the Saints were on the move. They did not go up into Wisconsin, but found a region in the northern part of Ray County where they could settle. Seven men who gathered the honey of wild bees lived there, but they were willing to sell out, since the honey was about gone. The settlement was made along Shoal creek, and though the country was not fertile or beautiful, the Saints knew it would become so through their labors and the blessing of God.

By December so many had come that they prayed the legislature to make a new county of the Shoal creek district. This was done, and it was named Caldwell. By April of the year 1837, a townsite for Far West had been chosen and surveyed, and lots were put up for sale. In July the ground was broken and prepared for the building of a temple. It was never finished; Missouri was not worthy of a temple then, but not long hence and the great House of God will be built there. In November, Far West was enlarged to include two square miles, and by this time the country was being rapidly settled and put under cultivation.

While the Saints in Missouri were showing the world an example of courage and industry seldom equaled, matters were not at a standstill at Kirtland. Few years in the history of the Church had been happier than the year 1836—the temple was dedicated, the Elders endowed and sent out to preach, Joseph went on a successful mission to the East, and converts were being made very fast. Among these were John Taylor, Lorenzo Snow and Willard Richards.

Elder Taylor received the truth from Parley P. Pratt who had been sent to Toronto, Canada. Previous to starting upon this mission, Heber C. Kimball, filled with the spirit of prophecy, came to Brother Pratt's house one night, woke him up, and made a prediction concerning the success that would attend him. He also promised that if he obeyed, his wife would be healed and bear a son. Brother Pratt did obey, and this was all fulfilled. Elder Taylor had been a Methodist minister, but refused to stop preaching what he believed to be true, and was reduced to the position of a member. After a thorough investigation of the Gospel he was baptized and never once wavered in his faith. John Taylor was born November 1, 1808, in Milinthorpe, England. He received a good education and when only seventeen years old he became a preacher. He came to America when he was about twenty-four, and settled in Canada, where he heard and accepted the Gospel.

Lorenzo Snow was born April 3, 1814, in Mantua, Portage County, Ohio. He was on his way to Oberlin college when he was first impressed with the Gospel. He happened to meet David W. Patten, and in talking with him grew much interested in religious ideas. Af-

8

ter Elder Snow had finished his work at college, on the advice of his sister, Eliza R. Snow, who had already joined the Church, he came to Kirtland to study Hebrew. Soon after this he became convinced of the truth of the Gospel, and joined the Church. He was baptized by Apostle John F. Boynton, in June, 1836, and not long after was ordained an Elder and began his life work in the ministry of our Savior.

Dr. Williard Richards, who became an Apostle and also second counselor to Brigham Young, was baptized on the last day of the year 1836. Heber C. Kimball and others spent the afternoon in chopping a large hole in the ice, and Brigham Young performed the ceremony. Brother Richards first heard of the Gospel when he happened to pick up and open carelessly a Book of Mormon. Before he read half a page he declared, "God or the devil had a hand in that book, for man never wrote it." He read it twice in about ten days and then, after selling his medicine and settling his accounts, traveled seven hundred miles to Kirtland to study the Gospel more closely. He soon came to the knowledge of the truth and asked for baptism, though in the dead of winter.

And thus the faithful boughs were being found and they soon brought forth blossoms that ripened into richest harvest.

CHAPTER XXV.

1836-37.

FOR some time previous to the year 1837 there was a fever raging over the United States. It was not a sickness that hurt the body, but the fever to buy for little and sell for much, and thus grow suddenly rich. It was the fever of speculation. Railroad engines had just been invented and were so successful that almost everybody who had money or could borrow it wished to buy railroad stock and make his fortune at once. People began moving out westward to the fertile lands of the Mississippi valley, and those who could lay their hands on money bought large tracts of land, hoping by the rise of prices to make immense profits. At this time, too, President Andrew Jackson, in order to destroy the national bank, took away the public money and placed it in private banks. This made it easier to borrow and speculation was consequently increased.

In 1836 the Prophet Joseph and other leading men in the Church, desiring to aid the business of the Saints in a proper way, established a kind of bank called the Kirtland Safety Society. In the beginning of 1837 actual business was started up and for a time all went well. But after a while the spirit of the land seized many of the brethren and they began to speculate wildly. Joseph saw that this would lead to evil and ruin, and he gave them serious warning. At length, unwilling to support anything that was not carried on in righteousness, he broke off all connection with the society.

The natural result of the speculation in this country came in 1837. It was a financial crash and such as the people of the United States have never known at any other time. Land and railroad stock and other kinds of property would rise no higher in price and began to come down. Men grew frightened and tried to sell, but others were frightened and would not buy, so those who held the stocks were ruined, as most speculators are sooner or later. Many banks failed because they had used the money that people had put in and could not pay it back. The Kirtland Safety Society also failed. Warren Parrish had stolen twenty thousand dollars or more from it, and other apostates and enemies of the Church fought against it. Many of the brethren, however, spent all they had to pay its debts.

This speculation and the failure and ruin that followed it, caused many men to apostatize from the Church and become bitter enemies to Joseph. He had warned them, but the lust for riches had filled their souls, driving out the Spirit of God, and they rejected his counsel. Yet the Prophet was blamed for the failure of the bank, when this was caused by their own mistakes and dishonesty.

Kirtland seemed to be, and no doubt was, filled with devils who were making every effort to overthrow the Church. It was at this time that the Lord directed Joseph to call Heber C. Kimball on a mission to England. Of course Brother Kimball accepted this new work. He was a man who never flinched before a duty. Orson Hyde and Williard Richards, learning that he was called, asked to be sent also. On the thirteenth of June, 1837, they departed from Kirtland, and on July 1st, accompanied by John Goodson, Isaac Russell, John Snider and Joseph Fielding, sailed from New York.

The good ship *Garrick* carried them safely across the great Atlantic, and just as the anchor was being lowered in the river Mersey, on the morning of July 20th, up sailed the *South America,* which left New York at the same time under a bet of ten thousand dollars. So you see the ship that carried the Elders won. Some of the brethren hastened to shore in a rowboat, and when they drew near, Heber C. Kimball with a great spring reached the landing and stood upon the soil of England, the first man bearing the holy Priesthood to set foot upon a foreign land in this dispensation.

The Elders were now at Liverpool, but they took stage at once for Preston, about thirty miles distant. As they alighted from the coach, they found themselves beneath a waving flag on which was written, "Truth will prevail." Queen Victoria had just been seated on the throne, and an election was being held for members of Parliament. The flag was in honor of the event, but the brethren took it as a sign of comfort for them and hoped and believed with all their hearts that the words would be fulfilled.

Sunday morning, July 23rd, Rev. James Fielding, brother of Joseph Fielding, gave it out in his meeting that some ministers from America would speak in the afternoon at his chapel. The brethren had not asked this favor and were very grateful for the offer. Elders Kimball and Hyde spoke, and another meeting was held at night. A third meeting was held the following Wednesday night and then Mr. Fielding closed his doors to the Elders. They met, however, at private houses and the work was not hindered. Only a week had passed when nine persons were ready for baptism.

That morning Elder Russell was to speak, but upon arising from his bed he was so afflicted with evil spirits that he felt he would die unless relieved. He came to Elders Kimball and Hyde and they administered to him, but while doing so Brother Kimball was knocked senseless to the floor by some unseen power. He was laid on the bed and prayed for, but the pain was so great that he could not lie down. He fell upon his knees and besought God to hear him.

The eyes of the Elders were opened then, and they saw about them a legion of devils, having the form of men but showing fiendish hatred in their faces. For an hour and a half these gnashed their teeth and foamed at the mouth and tried to come near the brethren, but seemed held back by some power. The Elders did not see the Lord, but the Prophet told them later that He was there protecting them from harm. With all their efforts, the evil spirits did not prevent the nine baptisms that Sabbath morning. Neither did they hinder the work of the English mission, for it prospered exceedingly, and when a general conference was held the following Christmas day in the "Cock Pit," at Preston, the Church in England numbered about one thousand souls.

CHAPTER XXVI.

1837-38.

WHILE these important things were going on in England, Joseph, with Sidney Rigdon and Thomas B. Marsh, left Kirtland for a visit to the Saints in Canada. When they reached Painesville, a few miles distant, their enemies held them all day by bringing lawsuits against Joseph on trumped-up charges. The sheriff said to Anson Call, who was present, "We don't want your Prophet to leave Kirtland, and he shan't leave;" but Brother Call went on Joseph's bond for seventeen hundred dollars, and he was able to go the next day. Part of the journey was made by steamer on Lake Erie and the brethren slept on deck with valises and boots for pillows, but they had health and clear consciences and slept in peace.

They spent a happy month traveling among the Canadian branches of the Church and associating with John Taylor and the other Saints. On their way back, in the latter part of August, Joseph and Sidney came by wagon from Buffalo to Painesville. While eating supper at the house of Mr. Bissell, who had been Joseph's lawyer, they discovered that a mob had gathered, and soon learned that the object was their murder. Their host was a true friend, however, and slipped them away by a back path. As soon as the mob found they were gone, bonfires were lit and sentinels placed along the Mentor road. But Joseph and Sidney took

to the swamps and the bonfires only helped them find
their way.

Sidney, being sick, was soon worn out, so Joseph
lifted him on his back and waded for hours through
mud and water carrying him. What a body and soul
that Prophet had! He would not desert a friend,
though he risked his life to save him, and with strength
like Samson's he carried him mile after mile through
darkness and swamps. They reached Kirtland in safety late at night, and the next day being Sunday, Joseph
preached a powerful sermon to the Saints.

It was a very sad home-coming for the Prophet.
The spirit of apostasy was very strong, and some of the
leading men were found in sin. On the 3rd of September fellowship was withdrawn from three of the
Apostles, Lyman and Luke Johnson and John F.
Boynton, and Frederick G. Williams was not sustained
as counselor to Joseph. At the same conference Oliver
Cowdery, Hyrum Smith, John and Joseph Smith, Sen.,
were made assistant counselors to the Prophet. A
week later the three Apostles confessed and were received back, but their repentance was very shallow as
it later proved.

Joseph spent most of October on a journey to Missouri. Sidney was with him and their special mission,
besides visiting the Saints, was to pick out places for
the eastern brethren to settle upon with their families
and make homes. The time had about come when Kirtland should be left and the Saints be gathered in one
place. A conference was held on the 7th of November,
soon after they came to Far West, and the Missouri
Saints rejected Frederick G. Williams, and Hyrum
Smith was made second counselor to Joseph.

The Prophet reached Kirtland in December and

the condition there was terrible. Warren Parrish, John F. Boynton, Luke Johnson, Joseph Coe and others had laid a plot to destroy the Church. These men who had received the most glorious visions of heaven now denied the faith and said Joseph was a false and fallen Prophet. Such men as Brigham Young were true to him and declared that they knew through the inspiration of the Holy Ghost that Joseph was a Prophet of God. This brought persecution upon them, and Brigham was compelled to flee for his life, soon after Joseph came.

Late on the night of the 12th of January, 1838, Joseph and Sidney saddled their horses and rode away from Kirtland. All through that winter night they rode and did not stop until sixty miles lay between them and their enemies. The life of a Prophet is not the easiest in the world, is it? They waited there for their families and again began their flight. For two hundred miles human blood-hounds from Kirtland tracked them, but the Lord blinded their eyes and the Prophet and his party went on unharmed. He reached Far West two months later. Some of the brethren had gone one hundred and twenty miles to meet him and bring him in comfort to Zion.

In the west as well as in the east, leading men of the Church had sinned and fallen. Soon after Joseph's coming Oliver Cowdery, David Whitmer, Lyman Johnson and William E. McLellin were cut off the Church. These, with Luke Johnson and John F. Boynton, made two of the three witnesses and four of the Twelve Apostles that had proved unfaithful. Some time later, on the 8th of July of this year, John Taylor, John E. Page, Wilford Woodruff and Willard Richards were called by revelation to be Apostles in the places of the fallen ones.

During the spring and summer the Prophet was busy forming stakes and providing for the Saints that were coming from Kirtland where confusion and violence reigned even in the Temple. On the sixth of July five hundred and fifteen of the faithful set out for Missouri under the leadership of the Seventy quorums. The third number of the *Elders' Journal* was published by Joseph at Far West in July. This was a paper that had been begun when the *Messenger and Advocate* was stopped. During this same month the great law of tithing was given to the Saints. It is recorded in the one hundred and nineteenth section of the Doctrine and Covenants, and being very short, all of you should read it. This law was given because the Saints would not obey the law of consecration, which was a higher law. The Lord still requires us to obey the law of tithing, but after a time if we are worthy we may be called to consecrate all we have to Him and hold our possessions as stewardships.

Joseph Smith's House at Far West.

CHAPTER XXVII.

1838.

THE LAST MISSOURI PERSECUTION BEGINS—FIFTEEN BRAVE MEN DEFEAT ONE HUNDRED AND FIFTY COWARDS—PENNISTON AND BLACK SWEAR FALSE-HOODS—JOSEPH AND LYMAN WIGHT PUT UNDER BONDS—MOB GATHERS.

AND now our story plunges into the awful events that began in August, 1838, and did not end until the spring of 1839—the time during which the Latter-day Saints were driven from Missouri. How much dreadful history was made in those dark months! How many men showed the rottenness of their hearts; and how many men and women showed the unutterable suffering they would endure for the sake of truth! It was a time when some did things that will send their souls to the most frightful places in hell, and when others earned a place among the companions of God.

At this time the Latter-day Saints numbered about fifteen thousand souls, and were settled mainly in Cald-well, Daviess and Carroll Counties. The sixth of August, 1838, was election day, and about twelve of the brethren went to the polls at Gallatin, Daviess County, to cast their votes. William Penniston, an old enemy of the Saints, who was running for one of the offices, made a violent speech in order to drive them from the polls. Some of his drunken friends attacked the breth-ren, but the brave twelve fought like lions with only their bare fists. Some of them were badly wounded but they pounded the heads of the Missourians so hard that the whole one hundred and fifty backed off and ran home for their guns. When they saw the mob gathering, the brethren hurried away. They hid their families in the hazel bushes and stood guarding them all night long in the rain.

A terrible story came to Far West the next morning that the mob had killed some of the brethren and would not give up their bodies. Joseph gathered about twenty trusty men and started at once for Daviess County. When they learned no lives were lost they were filled with joy. Matters, however, were bad enough and they continued on their way, determined to do all they could for the Saints.

They met a number of leading men of the county at Adam-ondi-Ahman, and made with them a covenant of peace. Before returning home they also called on Adam Black, a justice of the peace. They knew he was aiding the mob and wished to persuade him to deal justly with the Saints. He was one of those who had sold land to our people, and, like the others, wished to get it back without paying for it. They talked earnestly with him and then asked what he would do in the future. This is the answer he, of his own free will, wrote out to them.

I Adam Black a justice of the peace of Daviess County do hereby Sertify to the people coled Mormin, that he is bound to suport the constitution of this State, and of the United State, and he is not attached to any mob, nor will not attach himself to any such people, and so long as they will not molest me, I will not molest them. This 8th day of August 1838.

Adam Black, J P.

These movements toward peace did not please the mob at all. They thought to themselves, "How can we get our land back and drive away these cursed 'Mormons' if we agree to be at peace with them?" So Penniston swore before Judge Austin A. King that Joseph Smith and Lyman Wight had come into Daviess County with a great force of men to drive away all the old settlers. The sheriff was immediately sent to arrest them and was much surprised to find Joseph at home in Far West awaiting him. He was so struck with the gentleness of the Prophet that he refused to make the arrest, saying that he could act as officer only in his own county.

Although Adam Black had been ashamed of his meanness when the Prophet Joseph looked upon him with those clear, steady eyes that at other times had seen angels and even God Himself, yet when alone he was angry at himself and sought revenge. He swore that Joseph with one hundred and fity men had come to his house and said they would kill him that instant unless he signed a paper for them.

Lilburn W. Boggs was now governor of the state, and when he heard what Adam Black said he ordered out the state soldiers to restore peace. Joseph knew this would mean destruction to the innocent Saints, so on the thirtieth of August he offered himself to be tried in Daviess County in order to spare them. Lyman Wight followed his example.

That very day he and Sidney Rigdon began to study law under Generals Atchison and Doniphan, who, you remember, had been engaged as lawyers by the Saints in the first Missouri troubles. These men, besides being prominent lawyers, were generals in the state militia. You will hear much of them later. The Prophet no doubt thought that law would be a good thing to understand, since he was being arrested so often, and he showed his industry and calmness in beginning it now when so many dangers were about him.

The trial was held on September 7th. Adam Black swore to all manner of lies, and this of course made him guilty of perjury. Honest men bore witness that Joseph and Lyman were innocent, and Judge King admitted it outside of court, and yet to satisfy the mob, he put them under $500 bonds to keep the peace. These they furnished and went home. Two days later, Captain William Allred found three men taking guns, powder and shot from Ray County to the mob in Daviess. He arrested them and you may be sure the mob were much disappointed when their arms and ammunition did not come.

The mob had come together at a place near Millport and were making all kinds of threats against the Saints. Our people had made up their minds to defend themselves, and Lyman Wight was made commander of the forces. The mob tried all kinds of tricks to get the Saints to open the attack in order to get help from Governor Boggs. They took some of the brethren prisoners and gave it out that they were torturing them. This trick did not work, so William Dryden, a justice of the peace, complained that George A. Smith and Alanson Ripley would not allow themselves to be arrested and brought before his court. This was not true but it served as an excuse for Boggs to flood the state soldiers into Daviess County.

General Doniphan came first. He marched to the camp of the mob and ordered them to disperse. They promised to do so, but did not keep their word. He then went to the camp of the Saints and they offered to give up all who might be thought guilty of crime and go home peacefully, if the mob would break up. This is all that they could have been asked to do, and General Doniphan seemed satisfied. General Atchison came into Daviess County at this time, and, after learning the

conditions, he wrote to Governor Boggs that peace
would soon be secured. But the governor, who had
listened eagerly to all the lies that were being told, ordered up four more generals and heavy troops. General Parks, one of the four, though an enemy of the
Saints, wrote to Boggs saying that the Saints were
trying only to protect themselves. Lyman Wight and
fifteen or twenty others were called to appear at court
three weeks later, and peace seemed to have been established.

CHAPTER XXVIII.

1838.

MOB ATTACKS DE WITT—JOSEPH TRIES IN VAIN TO SAVE
THE TOWN—MOB DRIVEN AWAY FROM ADAM-ONDI-
AHMAN—APOSTLE PATTEN KILLED IN BATTLE OF
CROOKED RIVER—EXTERMINATION BEGINS AT
HAUN'S MILL—ALMA SMITH'S WOUND AND HIS
MOTHER'S FAITH.

ALTHOUGH the mob had not been able to fall upon
the Saints in Daviess County at this time, they
loved blood and plunder too well to remain at peace.
On the second of October the very same men who had
begun and kept up the trouble at Daviess, were found
gathered around the little town of De Witt, Carroll
County, under the leadership of Dr. Austin, Major Ash-
ley, a member of the legislature, and Rev. Sashiel
Woods, a Presbyterian clergyman. They were armed
with muskets and cannon, and opened fire upon the
town. The next day General Parks, with two com-

panies of militia, joined them. Bogart, one of the cap-
tains, was a rank enemy of the Saints, and the soldiers
themselves were in close sympathy with the mob.

After bearing the fire of the enemy for two days,
the Saints, who were under the command of Col.
George M. Hinkle, returned it. Though the mob numbered more than our people in De Witt, they dared not
continue the fight until more of their kind should join
them. When General Lucas heard that several persons
had fallen in this battle, he wrote to the governor that
if one of the citizens of Carroll had been killed, before
five days five thousand volunteers would be raised
against the "Mormons," and those base and degraded
beings will be exterminated from the face of the earth."

News came to the Prophet that his brethren in
Carroll County were in danger, and he hurried away
with all possible speed toward De Witt. It seemed as
though he was rushing on to death, for his journey lay
among his bitterest enemies, and the roads to De Witt
were guarded by those who would have loved to take
his life. But his own danger was nothing to him, he
knew that he could give new hope and courage to the
Saints, although he did not bear arms. He asked the
judges of the circuit court and other officers for protection to the Saints, but this was useless. Through his
efforts also, a number of honorable men made sworn
statements to the governor that the Latter-day Saints
were innocent and yet were being treated like enemies.
Boggs, however, would not let the state's forces interfere.

The mob was still afraid to make an open attack,
feeling it safer to starve the Saints out. They burned
our people's houses and killed and roasted their cattle,
while the owners were dying of hunger in the town. It
was useless to hold out any longer, and the Saints

agreed to leave, provided they were paid for their homes and property. They did leave, but received nothing. It was a terrible flight from De Witt to Far West, for the mob would not let them go in peace as they agreed. One poor mother, with a baby only a day old, tried to follow her friends, but the hardships were too great. Before they reached Far West she died and was buried, as were many others during that flight, without a coffin, at the roadside.

After they had gone the Rev. Mr. Woods invited his friends to go with him to Daviess County and drive the Saints from Adam-ondi-Ahman. He said that the land sales were near at hand, and if their luck was as good as at De Witt they could buy back for almost nothing the land they had sold to the "Mormons" only a short time before. When Joseph heard they were coming he again sought the post of danger and was with the Saints when the attack was made.

The mob, numbering nearly a thousand, plundered the farms that were some distance from the town. Men, women and children were out in the terrible storms of the 17th and 18th of October, without any homes to shelter them. Agnes Smith was one of these. Her husband, Don Carlos Smith, Joseph's brother, was on a mission. After her house had been burned, she fled from the mob with her two babies in her arms, and waded Grand river before she stopped to rest. But now General Parks sent Lyman Wight, who was one of his colonels, to lead a company of brethren against the cowards. The mobs fled but burned their huts as they went, and then spread the lie that the "Mormons" had done it. From this time on the people living in the scattered settlements made their way as soon as possible to Far West.

On the 24th of October, 1838, Captain Bogart,

9

who was a Methodist preacher when the more important work of killing and plundering the Saints did not call him away, led his mob-soldiers into camp on Crooked river. They had taken three brethren prisoners from their peaceful homes, and spread the report that they would murder them that night. When this came to Far West, Col. Hinkle sent David W. Patten with fifty men to the rescue. They reached Bogart's camp at daybreak, and as they marched down the hill, their forms, outlined against the sky, made a fine target for their enemies, hidden under the trees below.

Bogart's men suddenly opened fire. Three or four of the brethren fell. Captain Patten gave the order to shoot and then charge down upon the enemy. For a few minutes they fought hand to hand with swords, and then the mob, though larger in numbers, wheeled about and fled. As they ran, one turned and shot Captain Patten, giving him a mortal wound. That night he died, surrounded by the Prophet and his true friends. His last words to his wife were: "Whatever else you do, do not deny the faith!" Thus passed away Apostle David W. Patten, who had rescued friends and given up his life in doing so, and greater love than this no man hath.

This battle gave an excuse for the wild and terrible stories that set all Missouri in an uproar. Many good citizens were really afraid that the "Mormons" were about to march upon and destroy them. But surely Governor Boggs could not have been deceived, and yet he ordered out two thousand men with the command to kill off all the "Mormons" or drive them from the state.

This extermination, as it was called, began at Haun's Mill, in Caldwell County, on the 30th of October. The little settlement of Saints was at peace when suddenly two hundred and forty men rode up on horeseback and began shooting without a moment's warning. They showed no pity, but killed men, wounded women, blew out the brains of children that were pleading for their lives, and even robbed the dead. Seventeen were killed that afternoon, but there was no time to dig their graves. Amid the groans and tears of widows and fatherless children, their bodies were thrown into an old well and there they lay, a foul blot upon the land of liberty.

Little Alma Smith, who was only eight years old, after seeing his father and brother shot, fell to the ground with his hip joint and all the flesh about it torn away. He knew that if he cried out or asked for mercy, as his brother had done, the bad men would kill him. So he lay pretending to be dead until after dark, when he heard his mother call him. She placed him beside his dead father and brother and prayed that she might know what to do for her little boy. Our Father in heaven heard and answered her prayer. A voice told her to wash the wound clean with water in which the wood ashes from the fire had been soaked. She obeyed, although the cloth brought out each time mashed bone and flesh. After it was clean the voice told her to gather the roots of a slippery elm tree, make a poultice with them and fill the great hole in her boy's hip. Willard Smith, another son, who had escaped, gathered the roots and his mother made the poultice. Their prayers and faith were rewarded. Alma was healed and grew once more well and strong.

CHAPTER XXIX.

1838.

DURING the time of trouble in Missouri Satan
gained control over the hearts of some of the
leading men in the Church. Thomas B. Marsh, President of the Twelve Apostles, became an apostate and
joined William E. McLellin and other men who had
denied the faith, in spreading evil reports concerning
Joseph and the Church. How awful it was for these
men who had seen the most glorious sights that men on
earth have ever been permitted to see, now trying to
stir up the spirit of murder against the Prophet and to
destroy the Church of Christ!

Satan found other men also that were useful aids
to him in the great war he was waging. The highest
men in the state became his tools. Governor Boggs,
when the Saints appealed to him for help as the mob
was gathering about De Witt, said that the quarrel was
between the "Mormons" and the mob and they must
fight it out. But as soon as our people showed that they
would fight for their lives, he brought out the whole
power of the state to crush them, and Haun's Mill mas-
sacre was the first result.

On the day of that terrible slaughter the army

came before Far West and camped at a safe distance. In the morning a white flag was carried toward the town, and Col. Hinkle went out to meet it. When he returned he told Joseph that the commanders wished him and other leading men to come to their camp that night and see if they could not come to some terms of peace. The brethren agreed, but when they reached the camp they found the whole army awaiting them, and Hinkle, the traitor, said: "These are the prisoners I agreed to deliver up." The mob yelled with delight and General Lucas brandished his sword, as though he had done a very honorable thing.

Next morning, after having spent a cheerless night, the brethren were tried by court-martial. There were seventeen preachers of the different churches among the officers of this court. Joseph and some of the others were not soldiers and could not be tried legally by a soldier's court. Yet without being able to say a word for themselves they were condemned to be shot at eight o'clock the following morning on the public square of Far West. General Doniphan said boldly that it was murder, and that he washed his hands of the whole affair.

It was not enough for General Lucas to take the leaders by deceit, but this same day he commanded the people to give up their arms. They had to obey. Then followed such a scene as that at Independence just five years before, when the Saints surrendered their arms to Colonel Pitcher at his command. The mob militia was turned loose upon the helpless ones. They robbed the houses, and hunted down and shot the men. One woman also was killed and many others suffered a fate worse than death.

The Prophet and his companions were not shot. The vain Lucas wished to take them through the counties and show them as great prizes of war. They were permitted only to see their families, and when Joseph asked the guards to allow him to speak a few moments alone with his wife, they refused. The heartless wretches dragged their prisoners away and their wives and children cried as if their hearts would break, for they never expected to see them again.

Lucas took them direct to Jackson County, where they arrived on the fourth of November. A great crowd met them at Independence, and one woman asked the guard which was the Lord whom the "Mormons" worshiped. The Prophet was pointed out to her and she asked him whether he really called himself the Lord and Savior. He answered that he was only a man sent by Jesus Christ to preach the Gospel. She was surprised and asked more questions, and the Prophet that Sunday morning stood up and preached a powerful sermon on the first principles of the Gospel. This fulfilled a prophecy, for he had said publicly several months before that one of the Elders would preach in Jackson County before the close of 1838. During the four days that the brethren were at Independence. people flocked to their prison to hear them preach and became very friendly.

General Clark had been put in command of all the troops by Governor Boggs, because Clark was so heartless. He was jealous of Lucas because, having reached Far West first, Lucas had captured the Prophet, so he sent a command that the prisoners be brought to Richmond, Ray County, at once. But now arose a strange difficulty. The soldiers had become so friendly to the brethren that they would not take them back to Clark. At last three men were induced to go and they started out with their seven captives. On the way, however, they became so drunk that they could not care for themselves, and the prisoners took away their guns and horses and kept them until they sobered up. Escape would have been easy, but the brethren hoped for a trial, and all they wished was a chance to prove themselves innocent. When they reached Richmond they were chained together and day and night were disgusted with the curses and filthy stories of the guards.

Parley P. Pratt says that one night while these vile creatures were telling how they had defiled wives and virgins and dashed out the brains of men, women and children, Joseph arose and in a voice of thunder spoke:

"Silence! Ye fiends of the infernal pit! In the name of Jesus Christ I rebuke you, and command you to be still; I will not live another minute and hear such language Cease such talk, or you or I die this instant!"

He ceased to speak. He stood erect in terrible majesty Chained, and without a weapon, calm, unruffled and dignifide as an angel, he looked down upon the quailing guards. whose knees smote together, and who, shrinking into a corner, or crouching at his feet, begged his pardon, and remained quiet until exchange of guards.

I have seen ministers of justice, clothed in ministerial robes, and criminals arraigned before them. while life was suspended upon a breath, in the courts of England; I have witnessed a congress in solemn session to give laws to nations; I have tried to conceive of kings, of royal courts, of thrones and crowns; and of emperors assembled to decide the fate of kingdoms. But dignity and majesty have I seen but once, as it stood in chains, at midnight, in a dungeon, in an obscure village of Missouri

After Joseph and his companions had been taken by General Lucas to Independence, General Clark with about two thousand men came to Far West. This made six thousand soldiers that had preyed upon the little town during one week. He had all the brethren marched out and placed in line before him. They were perfectly harmless since their arms had been taken away. After putting fifty-six of them under arrest he commanded the remaining ones to prepare to flee from Missouri. He told them they need not hope ever to see their leaders again for their fate was fixed. After his speech he compelled the brethren, at the point of the bayonet, to sign deeds giving up their property to pay the expenses of the mob.

General Wilson had been sent to Adam-ondi-Ah-man. He put a guard around the town, arrested all the men and then tried them in a court of which Adam Black was judge. The men of the town were so manifestly innocent of wrong doing that even Adam Black would not convict them. Wilson ordered that within ten days they should all be gone from Daviess County.

Clark, with his fifty-six prisoners, came to Richmond to meet Joseph and the rest of the prisoners. He seems to have settled on their fate, for Elder Jedediah M. Grant heard him say to his soldiers: "Gentlemen, you shall have the honor of shooting the "Mormon" leaders next Monday morning at eight o'clock." But Clark was a great lawyer and knew that such action would be absolutely lawless. He therefore hunted for days to find some charge that he could make against his prisoners. In a letter to the governor, he said they were guilty of treason, murder, arson, burglary, robbery, larceny and perjury, but he decided to count mainly on treason and murder.

A mock trial was held for sixteen days, and at the end of this time all but eleven, including Joseph, Hyrum, Sidney Rigdon and Parley P. Pratt, were either let out on bail or discharged. Austin A. King was judge and let the worst falsehoods be given in testimony. The brethren were asked to call their witnesses. They named over fifty, and Bogart was sent out with a force of soldiers to bring them in. Instead of being put on the witness stand, however, they were thrown into prison. Whenever any witness showed that he would tell the truth about the prisoners the mob rushed upon him with their bayonets.

The condition of the Saints was now very, very dark. Joseph and his two counselors, Sidney and Hyrum, were put in Liberty jail, as it seemed, only to await death. Parley P. Pratt, one of the Apostles, was in prison at Richmond. David W. Patten had been killed, and Thomas B. Marsh, William E. McLellin and others of the Apostles, had denied the faith and become the bitterest enemies to the Church. The governor of the state had ordered the soldiers to slay the Saints. Winter was coming on, and once more they had to flee and find new homes.

CHAPTER XXX.

1838-39.

PETITION THE LEGISLATURE FOR JUSTICE—JOHN TAYLOR AND JOHN E. PAGE ORDAINED APOSTLES—PREPARATIONS TO LEAVE MISSOURI—TREATMENT OF JOSEPH AND HIS FELLOW-PRISONERS—ILLINOIS THE NEXT GATHERING PLACE OF THE SAINTS.

WHEN Joseph and his two counselors, Sidney and Hyrum, who formed the First Presidency of the Church, were thrown into prison, the Saints, though in great trouble, were not without a leader. Brigham Young was President of the Twelve Apostles, the quorum next in authority to the First Presidency. He gathered about him the faithful Apostles and brethren

and declared that he knew Joseph was a true Prophet.
He called all those whose faith was still strong to join
him in aiding the Saints. An earnest petition, telling
of the wrongs our people had suffered and asking for
justice, was sent to the legislature of Missouri. On the
19th of December this was discussed, and though
many of the members were honorable men and worked
hard for the cause of the Saints, yet those who had
helped in 'the outrages were too strong. The petition
was laid on the table, and this meant that nothing
would be done in the matter. On that very day John
Taylor and John E. Page were ordained Apostles under the hands of Brigham Young and Heber C. Kimball at Far West.

When it was found that the law-makers of Missouri would do nothing for the Saints, they knew they
must obey the command of Governor Boggs to leave.
Many of them were very poor. Their horses, cattle
and other animals had been shot or stolen, and their
homes taken from them. Some of the leading men
felt that every family should take care of itself, for
those best off were poor enough, but Brigham Young
declared that he would help the poor. He suggested
a pledge that all who had means would use it freely
until every worthy Saint who wished to go should be
taken from Missouri. Through his zeal many of the
brethren entered into this covenant and most were
faithful to it. When the mob saw that Brigham had
become a leader they began to persecute him as they
had done Joseph. In the middle of February, 1839,
he was compelled to flee from Far West.

The general movement of the Church had been
toward the west. You remember how the Saints gathered from New York to Ohio and from there went to
Missouri. But instead of continuing westward now,

Brigham and others traveled to the east, and, crossing over the Mississippi river, settled for a time in Quincy, Illinois, among a very friendly people. Although he himself had escaped, he did not forget the Saints that had been left behind and used all his efforts for their

BRIGHAM YOUNG.

aid. He worked so diligently for subscriptions that many of the brethren offered to sell their hats and clothing to raise money.

It was winter time, and the Missouri winters are very severe. The case of Amanda Smith is an instance of what the people suffered and did. Her husband and one son had been killed at Haun's Mill and another boy wounded as you no doubt remember. She had to milk, cut wood and do the work of a man. The mob swore they would kill the poor women and children who were left of this settlement if they did not leave the state. So she with her five children set out with an ox team. After unspeakable suffering she reached Quincy and then sent her wagon back for more of the Saints.

It was the last day of November, 1838, when Joseph and his companions were thrust into Liberty jail. The treatment they received was very harsh. At first they were not allowed to send or receive letters or see their friends. A number of times they were given poison, and once for five days a strange kind of meat was placed before them which the guards called "Mormon beef." Joseph warned the brethren not to eat of it since he believed it to be human flesh. After he was allowed to write he sent long letters of comfort, advice and instruction to the Saints. In one of these he said, "We glory in our persecution, because we know that God is with us. He is our friend, and will save our souls. We do not care for them that can kill our body; they cannot harm our souls. We ask no favors at the hands of the mobs, nor of the world, nor of the devil, nor of his emissaries the dissenters, and those who love, and make and swear falsehoods, to take away our lives."

In the early part of February, 1839, Sidney Rigdon was released by the court, but he dared not leave the prison because the mob many times had threatened to kill the brethren, should any court set them free. The jailer, however, was friendly, and let Sidney out secretly one night, and he escaped. Before going he showed a very bitter spirit, and went so far as to say that the sufferings of Jesus Christ were a fool to his. This was the spirit that began to destroy his usefulness and finally led to his fall.

At about this time Heber C. Kimball and Alanson Ripley were pleading with the judges at Liberty to give justice to their brethren. They were so earnest that at length one of the judges looked them squarely in the face and said to the others, "By the look of these men's eyes they are whipped but not conquered; and let us beware how we treat these men, for their looks bespeak innocence." The other judges had harder hearts and would not consent to set the prisoners free.

LIBERTY JAIL

As one of the brethren was moving his family eastward, he lost the road and instead of going into Illinois passed northward into Iowa. Here he met a certain Doctor Galland, who, learning the troubled story of the Saints, became much interested and began to plan to have them come and settle in the territory of Iowa. He owned a large tract of land and he offered to sell it to the Saints. Joseph learned of this while in prison, and though he could not investigate it he took a lively interest in the plan, for it offered a new place of gathering for the Church. Much land in Iowa was bought, and this called attention to the little town of Commerce, across the Mississippi river, where the Saints built the city of Nauvoo.

CHAPTER XXXI.

1839.

PRISONERS IN LIBERTY JAIL SEEK THEIR LIBERTY—TAKEN TO GALLATIN FOR TRIAL—ORDERED TO BE TAKEN TO BOONE COUNTY—THEIR ESCAPE FROM THE GUARDS—CONFERENCE AT FAR WEST—A PROPHECY FULFILLED—LAST OF THE SAINTS LEAVE MISSOURI.

TO KEEP the Prophet and his companions in prison and to refuse their many appeals to be tried by a fair court was so plainly unjust that some of them wished to escape if the Lord was willing. Joseph enquired, and the answer came that if all were agreed to leave that night the way should be opened for them

Lyman Wight, however, was fearful, and persuaded them to wait until the following night before trying to escape. They did so, but the Lord punished them for waiting. That night the jailor came in alone, leaving the doors open behind them, and they could easily have run out. The next night he came with a double guard, and also with some visitors, and when the brethren tried to escape they were stopped, and their visitors were locked up with them. When the Lord directs He wishes us to act at once. As soon as the people of the neighborhood learned that the prisoners had tried to break jail, they came rushing together and were very angry; but Joseph promised that no harm should be done, and their visiting brethren should not lose even a saddle blanket. This proved to be true.

On the 6th of April, 1839, the captives were taken from Liberty to Gallatin, Daviess County, for another trial before Judge King. They did not hope for justice from him. He was a brother-in-law to Hugh Brazeale, one of the men killed in the battle between the Saints and the mob in Jackson County, on the 4th of November, and he had a keen hatred for the "Mormons." At this time, too, fifty men of Daviess County had sworn that they would neither eat nor drink until they had slain Joseph Smith. Some of the brethren feared to go, but Joseph promised that if they would trust in the Lord He would preserve them, and they would receive better treatment than they had heretofore.

On reaching the courthouse the mob rushed upon them, but Joseph stepped out boldly and said, "We are in your hands. If we are guilty, we do not refuse to be punished by the law." Hearing this, the leaders held back their men. Joseph's promise came true. They were shown more kindness and were not injured,

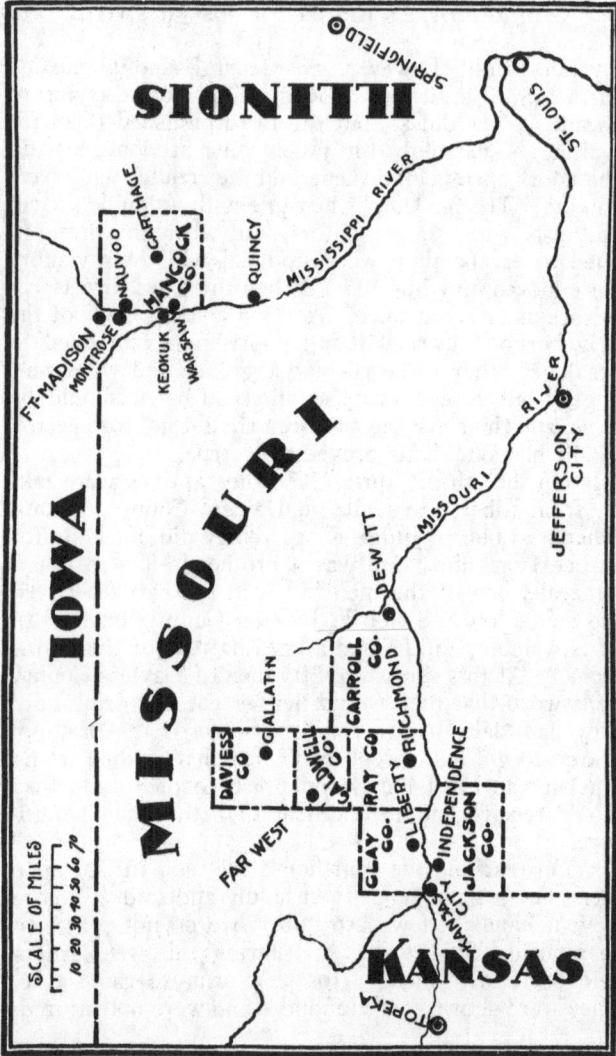

MAP SHOWING LOCATIONS OF THE LATTER-DAY SAINTS IN MISSOURI AND ILLINOIS.

but the trial did them no good. Judge King and the whole jury were drunk. Brother Stephen Markham, who had borne true witness, had to leave Gallatin in the night to save his life.

Judge King ordered that the prisoners be taken to Boone County, and on the way the guards became helplessly drunk. This time the brethren felt that the Lord had opened the way for them to escape. There was no justice in the courts for them. They had been put in prison and held there contrary to law, and they had a perfect right to escape and save their lives. This was on the 16th of April, and slowly and painfully they made their way toward the Mississippi. They traveled mainly at nights, crossed swollen streams, suffered for food and shelter, but through the mercy of God at length reached Quincy in safety, where they found most of the Saints.

A little before this last trouble for the Saints in Missouri began, on the 8th of July, 1838, Joseph enquired to find out the will of the Lord concerning the Twelve. He said that they should meet on the building spot of His house at Far West, on the 26th of the following April, and there take leave of His Saints. The apostates and enemies, knowing of this prophecy, swore that it never could be fulfilled. Far West was in their hands. There were few Saints there, and the enemies threatened to kill any of the Twelve if they made their appearance.

Brigham Young called the Apostles together and told them that they must fulfill the word of the Lord. They set out bravely for Far West, and on April 26th, 1839, before their enemies were awake, they met at the building spot of the Temple and held conference. They ordained Wilford Woodruff and George A. Smith to the Apostleship, cut thirty-one persons off the Church,

10

and dismissed their meeting. After saying good-by to
the Saints, they set out for Quincy. They had fulfilled a prophecy which the apostates sneeringly said
would prove Joseph a false prophet.

The remaining Saints now moved at once to Illinois, and the great crime against liberty was complete.
They had come to the new state full of hope and faith;
they left it bowed down in sorrow, but with faith un-

PRESIDENT WILFORD WOODRUFF.

changed. They parted from their homes and possessions, worth in all many millions of dollars. They left
the rough graves of their dear ones, whose bodies were
buried in many cases without coffins and whose souls
were crying from under the altar for the vengeance
of God.

CHAPTER XXXII.
1839-40.

SAINTS LOCATE AT COMMERCE, AFTERWARDS CALLED
NAUVOO—AN UNHEALTHY PLACE—A DAY OF MI-
RACULOUS HEALINGS—APOSTLES SET OUT UPON
MISSIONS TO ENGLAND—THEIR LABORS IN THAT
LAND.

WHEN the chosen people of the Lord had fled from
the wicked mobs of Missouri and settled among
the kind-hearted citizens of Illinois, they began to enjoy a season of welfare and happiness, that showed to
the world, after all the evil spoken of "Mormonism,"
how powerful this religion really is. This was one of
those times of peace that changed with the times of
trouble. And you have doubtless noticed since the organization of the Church that after a season of persecution comes a season of liberty.

This was the last time in the life of the Prophet
Joseph when he could use his great mind and soul un-
disturbed, to advance the people he was chosen to lead;
and though some troubles came to him, yet these were
small compared with what he had already passed
through. We love to look at the Prophet during this
time, in the prime of his manhood, employed at the
work that was so near his heart. The Church had

grown to number many thousands and its members were both in the new and in the old world. As the work grew, the burden on the Prophet became heavier, but he was equal to it all.

On May-day, in the spring of 1839, Joseph bought the first piece of land at Commerce, a little village of six houses on the banks of the Mississippi, about fifty miles north of Quincy. The ground was low and marshy, and the place very unhealthful, but it was a beautiful situation. The great Mississippi river flowed in a splendid curve on three sides of it. The name was soon changed from Commerce to Nauvoo, the latter being a Hebrew word, meaning beautiful. Ten days later, Joseph settled his family here, and the Saints began rapidly to gather and build up a city. They lived at first in tents and log-huts and were very glad of these.

Land was bought also just across the river in Iowa, and Brigham Young and others settled there. The Saints were all worn out with the great hardships of the past winter, and this made them an easy prey to the disease that lurked in the swamps along the river. It was not long until most of them were taken down with chills and fever. Joseph himself was stricken, his iron constitution giving way on account of nursing the sick about him so constantly.

On the 22nd of July the Prophet rose from his bed, and filled with the Spirit of the Lord he went forth, and these are some of the labors of that day as given by Wilford Woodruff, who was present at the time:

Many lay sick along the bank of the river, and Joseph walked along up to the lower stone house, occupied by Sidney Rigdon, and he healed all the sick that lay in his path. Among the number was Henry G. Sherwood, who was nigh unto death. Joseph stood in the mouth of his tent and commanded him in the name of Jesus Christ to arise and come out of his tent, and he obeyed him and was healed. Brother Benjamin Brown and his family also lay sick, the former appearing to be in a dying condition. Joseph healed them in the name of the Lord. After healing all that lay sick upon the bank of the river as far as the stone house, he called upon Elder Kimball and some others to accompany him across the river to visit the sick at Montrose. Many of the Saints were living at the old military barracks. Among the number were several of the Twelve On his arrival, the first house he visited was that occupied by Elder Brigham Young, the President of the quorum of the Twelve, who lay sick. Joseph healed him, when he arose and accompanied the Prophet on his visit to others who were in the same condition. They visited Elder W Woodruff, also Elders Orson Pratt and John Taylor, all of whom were living in Montrose. They also accompanied him. The next place they visited was the home of Elijah Fordham, who was supposed to be about breathing his last. When the company entered the room the Prophet of God walked up to the dying man, and took hold of his right hand and spoke to him; but Brother Fordham was unable to speak; his eyes were set in his head like glass, and he seemed entirely unconscious of all around him Joseph held his hand and looked into his eyes in silence for a length of time. A change in the countenance of Brother Fordham was soon perceptible to all present. His sight returned, and upon Joseph asking him if he knew him, he, in a low whisper, answered, "Yes." Joseph asked him if he had faith to be healed. He answered, "I fear it is too late; if you had come sooner I think I could have been healed." The Prophet said, "Do you not believe in Jesus Christ?" He answered in a feeble voice, "I do" Joseph then stood erect, still holding his hand in silence several moments, then he spoke in a loud voice, saying, "Brother Fordham, I command you in the name of Jesus Christ to arise from this bed and be made whole." His voice was like the voice of God and not of man It seemed as though the house shook to its very foundation. Brother Fordham arose from his bed and was immediately made whole. His feet were bound in poultices, which he kicked off; then putting on his clothes he ate a bowl of bread and milk and followed the Prophet into the street. The company next visited Brother Joseph Bates Noble, who lay very sick He also was healed by the Prophet.

By this time the wicked became alarmed, and followed the company into Brother Noble's house. After Brother Noble was healed all kneeled down to pray. Brother Fordham was mouth, and while praying he fell to the floor. The Prophet arose, and looking round he saw quite a number of unbelievers in the house, whom he ordered out. When the room was cleared of them Brother Fordham came to and finished his prayer.

Soon after this great day of healing, the Apostles began setting out on their mission to England. Heber C. Kimball had already opened the English mission in the summer of 1837, but he returned home the following year and Willard Richards was left in charge. We can hardly think of greater sacrifices that men can make than the Apostles made in going out at this time. Many were very sick and their families suffering from sickness and want. The Apostles traveled without purse or scrip, relying on the Lord to care for them and supply their wants. Their sufferings and integrity will be lessons of faith for all time to come.

On the first of July Joseph and his counselors crossed the Mississippi river to the Iowa shore and there held meeting with the Apostles. Joseph blessed them for their journey, and gave much instruction concerning their coming duties, and unfolded many of the glorious things pertaining to the Kingdom of God.

One week later John Taylor and Wilford Woodruff set out for their mission. Brother Woodruff rose from a sick bed, where his wife also lay unable to rise. He blessed her and went forth without a murmur. Elder Taylor was about the only one of the Apostles who enjoyed health, but on the way he too was stricken down. Although he was without money he would not give up, and the Lord rewarded his faith. He reached New York with only one cent in his pocket. The brethren there offered to donate enough to pay his passage to

England but he refused it, saying that the Lord would open the way. Before the day of sailing enough money was given him to pay for his own ticket and that of Brother Turley, whom he had promised to take with him.

Parley P. Pratt had escaped after great trouble from prison through the aid of his brother Orson, and now together, on the 29th of August, they left Nauvoo. On the 18th of September Brigham Young departed, though unable to walk alone, and leaving a sick wife and a baby only ten days old. He was joined by Heber C. Kimball, whose wife and all but one child were sick. Both Brigham and Heber were so weak that they could not carry their single trunk. George A. Smith went three days later, leaving father, mother, sister and brother helpless in a log stable. He was so thin and pale that a man called out as he passed, "Somebody has been robbing a graveyard of a skeleton."

Joseph said later that the Apostles "went forth weeping and bearing precious seed," but they "returned with rejoicing and bearing sheaves with them." It was a glorious work they did. Each one was blessed with success in his particular field. Willard Richards was ordained an Apostle on the 14th of April, 1840, and this made eight Apostles laboring in the British mission. In a little over one year 5,000 copies of the Book of Mormon had been printed, and 3,000 hymn books and 50,000 tracts had been published. The *Millennial Star,* a monthly paper, had been begun, with Parley P. Pratt as editor. Over 3,000 more persons had joined the Church, and the precious seed was sown in many parts of England, and also in Scotland, Ireland and the Isle of Man. And when the Apostles came back they did return with rejoicings and their sheaves were full of precious grain.

CHAPTER XXXIII.

1839-40.

WHEN the government of the United States was
founded, the idea of the inspired fathers of the
nation was to make it possible for all men to enjoy liberty and justice. Each state had its government but
above the states was the national government, which
was to give justice when it could not be obtained in the
states. This was the idea Joseph the Prophet had of
our government, and he determined that since Missouri
would not right the great wrong done to the Saints, he
would carry their cause to the United States and there
seek justice. You know something of what they suffered. They lost their lands, houses, cattle and almost
all that they had, and worse than this, they were robbed
of their rights as American citizens to worship God as
they saw fit and to live peacefully wherever they chose
to live.

In the fall of 1839, in company with Elias Higbee
and Sidney Rigdon, Joseph went east to Washington to
lay the matter before the President and Congress, and
to ask that claims against Missouri for about one and

a half million dollars' worth of property be paid. While they were traveling by stage in the mountains between Philadelphia and Washington, the driver left his seat to get a drink of grog. The horses became frightened and began to run. The road led down a hill and the pace soon became terrific. The passengers were beside themselves with fear.

Joseph's presence of mind and cool bravery were at once seen. He calmed his fellow-travelers as well as possible, but had to hold one excited woman from throwing her baby out of the window. He then opened the door and securing a hold on the side of the coach, although the horses were running at full speed, drew himself by main strength up to the driver's seat. Gathering up the reins, he soon had the horses under control.

The passengers felt that they owed him their lives, and seemed very grateful. They praised his bravery, as it of course deserved, in the highest terms, and some of them who were members of Congress, said that they would speak of the act before that body, feeling sure that mention would be made of their deliverer. They asked his name, but when he told them he was Joseph Smith, all their gratitude and praise ceased at once, and nothing more was said.

Sidney had been left sick at Philadelphia, but Joseph and Judge Higbee, on the twenty-ninth of November, the day following their arrival at Washington, visited President Van Buren and gave him their letters of introduction. He read one, and looking up with a frown on his face said: "What can I do? I can do nothing for you. If I do anything I shall come in contact with the whole state of Missouri." Joseph was not frightened by such cowardly words and thought the man a fool for judging before he had heard their cause. He told the President boldly of how Missouri had over-ridden the Constitution and of the horrible crimes that resulted. Van Buren was moved to pity and promised to reconsider what he had said.

Joseph and his companion prepared a long petition to place before Congress. They met a committee of the representatives and senators from Illinois and other friendly congressman and laid their cause plainly before them. They again visited President Van Buren, but he had now turned against them and at this time spoke those cowardly, traitorous words: "Your cause is just, but I can do nothing for you. If I take up for you I shall lose the vote of Missouri."

The committee appointed by Congress to consider the petition reported against it also. For their own political reasons, like the President, they did not wish to favor the "Mormons," and besides this they probably feared to touch the great question of State's Rights, which was not settled until the Civil War.

Joseph's mission to Washington seemed to be in vain. Yet it was not entirely a failure. He preached a number of public sermons, and he did much to spread the truth, and gained many friends. He also had a chance to become acquainted with those who were in high places in the nation, and measure his strength and intelligence with theirs.

At the April conference of 1840, Apostle Orson Hyde, who had not gone with the other members of the Twelve to England, was called on a mission to Jerusalem. Apostle John E. Page was appointed to go with him, but this he refused to do. Elder Hyde left Nauvoo nine days later, traveled to the Holy Land and there offered a prayer of dedication on the Mount of Olives, that the Jews might gather home. He then went to Europe, and in Germany published a pamphlet telling of the rise and doctrines of the Church. His mission lasted over two years.

In midsummer of the year 1840, a circumstance happened which showed that the old spirit had not died out in Missouri. A party of men from that state came to Nauvoo and took away by force—actually kidnapped —four of the brethren. These were James Allred, Alanson Brown, Noah Rogers and Benjamin Boyce, and before they escaped they were nearly killed by the cruelties of the Missourians. Two or three months later, on the fifteenth of September, Governor Boggs asked Governor Carlin of Illinois to have Joseph Smith, Sidney Rigdon, Lyman Wight, Parley P. Pratt, Caleb Baldwin and Alanson Brown arrested for having fled from the Missouri prisons.

Although Governor Carlin must have known that the object of Boggs was murder, yet he issued an order for their arrest, and the sheriff was sent with it to Nauvoo. Joseph and the others who were there went into hiding, because they knew that if they were taken back to Missouri it meant foul play. The sheriff, therefore, returned the order to Governor Carlin. The danger was past and Joseph again came out among the people.

On the day before the order for the Prophet's arrest was made, Joseph Smith, Sen., the first Patriarch of the Church, died on account of the hardships he had endured in fleeing from Missouri. He was faithful to the last and died a martyr. On the twenty-fourth of January, 1841, Hyrum was appointed Patriarch, and William Law was made second counselor to Joseph in Hyrum's place.

Nauvoo had now grown, as if by magic, into a town of considerable size. Hundreds of comfortable houses had taken the place of the half dozen huts found in the marsh, a year and a half before. The citizens now asked the legislature that it be made into a city. Joseph and others wrote out a charter, and in December it was accepted by the legislature, and signed by the governor. This charter, as Joseph said, made it possible for any honest man to live secure, whatever his religion or party. It provided for a mayor, aldermen and councilors; also for a university and body of soldiers called the Nauvoo Legion.

An election was held on the first of February, and John C. Bennett, an educated man who had shortly before joined the Church, was elected mayor. Joseph was one of the councilors. At the first city council meeting the Prophet presented a bill for the organizing of a university, and he was elected one of the trustees. When the Legion was formed with six companies, Joseph was made lieutenant-general. So you see that the first President of the Church, as all the others have been, was a practical man, and was willing to do his part as a citizen.

He accepted the office of councilor, a somewhat humble position, because he wished to aid in giving the young city good government. At one of the first meetings he introduced a bill to prevent the sale of liquor, and this made drunkenness almost unknown. He accepted the position of trustee of the university because he was a great friend to education and wished to make the school thrive. He accepted the position of lieutenant-general in the Legion because it was a duty of the citizens to have a military organization; and he was willing to do his part to make it a worthy one.

CHAPTER XXXIV.

1841-42.

THE bright days of prosperity seemed to have come
to the Church with the spring of 1841. At a general conference held on the 6th of April, the corner
stones of the temple at Nauvoo were laid and three days
later Lyman Wight was ordained an Apostle. This
made the quorum of the Twelve complete. All the
other eleven were successfully engaged in the ministry.

When the summer came, Hyrum and William Law
went on a mission to the east, and Joseph went down
the Mississippi to Quincy with them. Governor Carlin
lived here and the Prophet visited him, and the two
men had a long friendly talk. The governor had commissioned Joseph lieutenant-general of the Nauvoo
Legion only three months before, and nothing was said
of the order for the arrest of the Prophet that had
been sent out in September of the preceding year.

After Joseph had set out for Nauvoo, Carlin
found the old order and put it into the hands of the
sheriff and sent him with a number of men, one of them
a Missourian, to capture the Prophet. They found and
arrested him about twenty-five miles from Nauvoo, but
when the man from Missouri began to threaten and
curse, most of those who had come with the sheriff,

being honorable men, withdrew and would have nothing to do with the arrest. Joseph went back to Quincy and his trial was set by Stephen A. Douglas for three days later, the 8th of June, at Monmouth, Warren County.

Sheriff King, who had made the arrest, went back with Joseph to Nauvoo, but on the way became very sick. The Prophet took him to his own home, and he himself nursed the officer most carefully. Early on the morning of the day before the trial, with about twenty good friends, Joseph started for Monmouth and reached there the following day. The people were very curious to see him. The different ministers had stirred up a great deal of hatred, and a mob tried to seize him but the sheriff kept them back. The trial did not take place that day and Joseph was held secure in prison until the 9th.

Six prominent lawyers, with bravery enough to defend an unpopular cause, appeared in court for Joseph, and they advanced two strong reasons why the Prophet should not be sent back to Missouri. The first one was that the order for arrest, having been sent out once and returned to Governor Carlin, became void and could not be served again; and the second was, that the action of Missouri had been illegal and the indictment of the Prophet was obtained through fraud and bribery. Stephen A. Douglas was the judge, and he ordered the Prophet to be set free on account of the reasons given. Many of the lawyers on the other side had been hired by religious people and some had even come from Missouri to take part in the case.

Mr. O. H. Browning, who later became secretary of the interior in President Johnson's cabinet, was the principal attorney for Joseph, and after arguing upon the points of law, he spoke of the injustice of sending the Prophet back to Missouri to be murdered by the ruffians of that state. He told of the sufferings the Saints had endured, and so pitiful was the story that many were weeping when he closed. These were the last words of his address:

Great God! have I not seen it? Yes, mine eyes have beheld the blood-stained traces of innocent women and children in the drear winter, who had traveled hundreds of miles barefoot through frost and snow, to seek a refuge from their savage pursuers. It was a scene of horror, sufficient to enlist sympathy from an adamantine heart. And shall this unfortunate man, whom their fury has seen proper to select for sacrifice, be driven into such a savage land, and none dare to enlist in the cause of justice? If there was no other voice under heaven ever to be heard in this cause, gladly would I stand alone, and proudly spend my last breath, in defense of an oppressed American citizen.

Elder Amasa Lyman, who was with Joseph at this trial, delivered a sermon at the request of a number of people, on the evening of this day, and a much better feeling for the Prophet and the Saints sprang up as a result. Many, of course, remained bitter and spread all kinds of lies concerning Judge Douglas and the trial, but all fair-minded people said that the decision was just. There was much rejoicing when the Prophet reached Nauvoo, for all expected that this would be the end of persecution from Missouri.

In July and the following months, six of the Apostles came home from their mission to England, and this brought joy to the heart of Joseph. The burden of governing the Church was growing very heavy, and he needed these true, prudent men about him to aid in the great work. They were all dear friends of his, and he bore them a love that only faithful followers of Jesus can feel for one another. But his happiness for their return and his release from danger was saddened by the death of Don Carlos, his youngest brother, who died on the 7th of August. When only fourteen years of age, this boy had begun his missionary work and traveled with his father preaching the Gospel. He had gone on other missions later and at the age of nineteen was ordained president of the High Priest's quorum. At the time of his death, in his twenty-sixth year, he was one of the city councilors and brigadier-general of the Nauvoo Legion.

About this time the Prophet was visited by a large band of Sac and Fox Indians. Some of them had read the Book of Mormon and wished to know more about the man who had interpreted this great record of their fathers. Joseph told them of the beginning of their people, and that God had promised they should be white and beautiful again when they became righteous. He counseled them to bury the hatchet forever and to live no more for war and slaughter but to turn to lives of peace. When he had finished, Keokuk, one of the chiefs, said, "I believe you are a great and good man; I look rough, but I also am a son of the Great Spirit. I have heard your advice; and we intend to quit fighting, and follow the good advice you have given us."

At a general conference, held in the grove at Nauvoo, beginning October 2nd and lasting for three days, the doctrine of baptism for the dead was publicly preached by the Prophet. This had been taught already to the Apostles and others, but not to the whole Church. The Saints were filled with joy when they learned that their fathers, mothers and other relatives and all the spirits that had passed away without a knowledge of the truth might yet receive salvation equal to their own. Some baptisms had already been performed, but now the Prophet said that there would be no more until they could be carried on in the temple. It was a month before the baptismal font was ready for use, and soon after it was dedicated by President Young, baptizing was again commenced.

In February, 1842, Apostles John Taylor and Wilford Woodruff began to publish *The Times and Seasons,* and in the next month Joseph became editor of this paper. This was the fourth Church paper that had been set up and published. In this same month of March, under the direction of the Prophet, the Female Relief Society of Nauvoo was founded. You all know how much good the Relief Societies are doing at the present time, and this was the first in the Church. Emma Smith, Joseph's wife, was made president, and Eliza R. Snow was secretary.

CHAPTER XXXV.

1842.

BENNETT'S PLOTS TO DESTROY THE PROPHET—A PROPHECY—JOSEPH CHARGED WITH BEING AN ACCESSORY TO THE ATTEMPTED ASSASSINATION OF BOGGS—HIS ARREST AND TRIAL—SET AT LIBERTY.

THERE are few things that will drive the Spirit of the Lord away from a man or woman or a boy or girl so quickly as impurity. Hundreds of men have fallen in this Church, some from the position of Apostles even, because they were not virtuous. There are few instances that illustrate this better than the fall of John C. Bennett. He was a man of great ability, had a good education and had become very prominent among the Saints. But he did not resist temptation, and the Spirit of God withdrew from him. Then he began to draw others into his wickedness. He told a number of men and women that the Prophet had said that the members of the Church need not be chaste. Some of them sinned with him. He even went further, and began plotting to kill Joseph.

Bennett was major-general of the Nauvoo Legion, and on the 7th of May, 1842, a sham battle was arranged, in which the twenty-six companies of the Legion, numbering two thousand men, were to take part. Joseph was lieutenant-general and he took his place with the visitors, in such a position as to be able to overlook the battle. Bennett, the traitor, tried to get him alone into a certain position in the ranks, where, as later turned out, he could be shot by some of Bennett's friends, and, amid the noise and smoke, the real person could never be told. The Spirit of the Lord prompted Joseph not to go, and revealed to him the wickedness of his former friend, so the plot failed. Shortly after this Bennett resigned his position as major and was cut off the Church, but with tears in his eyes he pleaded for his standing, and mercy was shown unto him.

After forgiveness had been given he went before Daniel H. Wells, who was not then a member of the Church, and stated upon his oath that Joseph had never taught him "anything contrary to the strictest principles of the Gospel, or of virtue, or of the laws of God or man, under any circumstance, or upon any occasion, either directly or indirectly in word or deed." He also made public confession of his wrongdoing and all the falsehoods he had told concerning the Prophet. It was not long, however, before he again fell into sin, and then he was cut off the Church and the world was warned against him as a wicked, impure man. He now turned his spite upon the Prophet and the Church and became the author of the most frightful lies. It was largely due to him that persecution again sprang up. John C. Bennett might have lived an honorable life, held important positions of trust and been a favored servant of God, if he had resisted temptation. He now became an enemy of the truth, was a murderer in his heart, and after a short life of crime, died a most wretched death.

One day Joseph crossed the Mississippi river from Nauvoo to Montrose, on the Iowa shore, in company with a number of prominent Free Masons. He was waiting for them in the shade of the Masonic building while they finished up their business on the inside, when the subject of the Missouri persecutions came up and Joseph made a prophecy. He said that the Saints would continue to suffer much affliction and would be driven to the Rocky mountains. Many would apostatize, others would be put to death or lose their lives through exposure and disease, but some of those present would live to go and help make settlements and build cities and see the Saints become a mighty people in the midst of the Rocky mountains. This prophecy was made on the 6th of August, 1842, five years before any Latter-day Saint ever saw the valley of the Great Salt Lake.

Two days after this, on the 8th of August, the Prophet and Orrin Porter Rockwell were arrested by the sheriff and two deputies of Adams County, on the charge of murder. Three months before, Lilburn W. Boggs was found one night lying in his bed at his home in Independence, Jackson County, with three bullet wounds in the head. These were not fatal and he soon recovered. The report was spread that the "Mormons" had done this to punish Boggs for the murders of the

Saints which he had set the mob to do; but there was
no evidence to show that any member of the Church
had been in the slightest degree connected with the
crime.   In the latter part of July, almost three months
after the shooting, Boggs swore out a complaint against
Orrin P. Rockwell for having tried to murder him, and
against Joseph Smith as his aid in the crime.

Boggs had applied to Governor Reynolds of Missouri, and Reynolds had applied to Governor Carlin of
Illinois, for the arrest of the Prophet and Brother
Rockwell as fugitives from justice.   Thousands of people had seen Joseph at Nauvoo on the day that Boggs
had been shot.   Certainly he had not been in Missouri,
and therefore had not fled from the state.   According
to his right, the Prophet demanded that they be taken
to the city court of Nauvoo for a hearing.   This the
officers refused to allow, but seeming not to know what
their duties really were, they went back to Quincy to
consult with Governor Carlin.   When they came back,
two days later, Brother Rockwell had gone east, and
Joseph had hid himself, not wishing to be taken, contrary to law, back to Missouri.   The sheriff tried to
frighten Emma into telling where Joseph was, by
threatening her if she refused, but it was of no use.

During more than four months the Prophet was
hiding at Nauvoo and the neighboring country, though
once he came suddenly before the people and preached
to them.   During this time he wrote important letters
to the Saints, especially on the subject of baptism for
the dead.   All kinds of tricks were tried in order to
capture him.   A reward of $1,300 was offered for his
arrest, and the threat was made that if he was not
found the mob would come upon Nauvoo and burn the
city.   On hearing this last, the Prophet told Wilson
Law, who had been made major-general, that though

the Saints would make every sacrifice that God or man could require at their hands to preserve peace, yet they should defend themselves if necessary.

At length, relying on the advice of Mr. Butterfield, an able lawyer who had become Joseph's attorney, and the promise of Thomas Ford, who had been elected governor of Illinois after the end of Carlin's term, the Prophet permitted himself to be arrested by Wilson Law on the 26th of December, and with a company of brethren, set out for Springfield, the capital of Illinois, to be tried before the circuit court.

On the last day of the year, 1842, the Prophet was released by Judge Pope on two thosuand dollars bonds to appear for trial the following week. The court house was crowded with people. Some were friendly to the Prophet and others were his enemies, but all wished to see him. After he was set free, he went to visit Governor Ford and on his way he passed between two walls of people. Soon after this a loose team went dashing past the State house and somebody called out, "Joseph Smith the 'Mormon' Prophet is running away." The legislature at once dismissed and the members came running out of doors to take part in the excitement. The Prophet had grown to be a very interesting person to them. Next morning being Sunday, the State house was offered for the purpose of holding a meeting. Orson Hyde and John Taylor preached to a great congregation.

The trial was held on the 4th of January, 1843, and after a powerful argument by Mr. Butterfield, Judge Pope decided that the whole action of the Missouri and Illinois officers, in trying to take the Prophet and carry him away for trial, was illegal. By this decision Joseph was given his liberty again. He returned to Nauvoo on the 10th of January and the

Saints were overjoyed to see him in safety again. The Twelve Apostles set apart the 17th of that month as a day of humility, fasting, praise, thanksgiving and prayer. This day was kept, and all were truly grateful to God for having preserved the Prophet's life. Next day Joseph and Emma gave a banquet to many of the Saints in honor of the fifteenth anniversary of their marriage.

CHAPTER XXXVI.
1843.

A BLOODY WAR PREDICTED—THE PROPHET'S INTERVIEW WITH STEPHEN A. DOUGLAS—A PROPHECY—THE CELESTIAL ORDER OF MARRIAGE—JOSEPH KIDNAPPED AND ABUSED—HE ENTERTAINS THE MEN WHO SOUGHT TO TAKE HIS LIFE.

WHEN Judge Pope declared that Joseph was a free man again after the trial at Springfield, on the fifth of January, 1843, a few months of peace followed his long hiding. It was a happy, busy time for the Prophet—a time when many prophecies were uttered by him and much precious truth given to the Saints. In the early part of this year there was a great stir made about the prophecy of a man named Miller who said that Jesus and the day of judgment were to come on April 3rd. A committee of young men came from New York to see Joseph about this, and he said positively that the Lord would not come in the year 1843 to reign in this world. At a later time in a conference, he declared to the Saints that Jesus would not come before he, Joseph, was eighty-five years old.

Orrin P. Rockwell was captured by the Missourians and thrown into prison in the month of March, and when the Prophet heard it, he prophesied in the most positive terms that Brother Rockwell would get away honorably from his captors.

One night about the same time Joseph, Wilford Woodruff and Willard Richards saw a great streak of light in the sky in the shape of a sword with the hilt downward. The Prophet told them that as sure as God sits on a throne in heaven, so sure would there be a bloody war, and the flaming sword was a certain sign thereof. A short time after this he repeated the prophecy that the bloodshed should begin in South Carolina.

On the eighteenth of May, Joseph passed through Quincy, and on the invitation of Stephen A. Douglas, stopped and dined with him. Judge Douglas asked for an account of the Missouri persecutions, and when Joseph finished it, Douglas spoke in the strongest terms against Boggs and the other officials and said that they should be punished. After dinner Joseph said to his host:

Judge, you will aspire to the presidency of the United States, and if you ever turn your hand against the Latter-day Saints, you will feel the weight of the hand of the Almighty upon you; and you will live to see and know that I have testified the truth to you, for the conversation, of this day will be with you through life.

The prophecy was fulfilled. Douglas did turn his hand against the Latter-day Saints, in the hope of winning favor thereby, and when he ran for president against Abraham Lincoln, in the fall of 1860, he was defeated, and soon after died.

A great trial came to the Prophet in the latter part of his life, and a very severe test was made of his willingness to obey the word of God unto him, relating to celestial marriage. Joseph at once began to teach

Hyrum and other faithful, true men the will of the
Lord. He told Emma, his wife. After a struggle she
consented that her husband take other wives, and she
herself gave them to him. Even then Joseph did not
think it wise to make the revelation public, and not
until the twelfth day of July was it written down. Just
one month later it was read before the High Council
at Nauvoo, by Hyrum Smith.*

The Prophet was not engaged entirely in spiritual
matters during the first half of 1843. He had been
elected mayor of Nauvoo, and gave much attention to
his various duties. He was full of life and vigor and
kept up his athletic practices. It was during this time
that he met William Wall, a champion wrestler of
Ramus, Illinois, and had a friendly bout with him.
It must have been a fine thing to see those two powerful men struggling with all the skill they had for
the mastery, but Wall had met a match and Joseph
came offer victor.

In the month of June a plot was laid for Bennett,
the apostate, and Samuel Owens, the old leader of
the Jackson County mobs, to bring Joseph back to
Missouri. They worked upon Governors Reynolds
and Ford; and two men, Sheriff Reynolds of Jackson
County and Sheriff Wilson of Hancock County, were
sent to capture him. The Prophet was visiting near
Dixon, about one hundred and fifty miles from Nauvoo, when two officers, disguised as "Mormon" mis-
sionaries, came to the house where he was staying and

*The passage of the anti-polygmay laws and the de-
cision of the Supreme Court of the United States, uphold-
ing them, resulted in 1890, during the presidency of Wilford Woodruff, in the suspension of the practice, and plural
marriage among the Saints is now neither taught nor practiced.—*Editor*

said, "We want to see Brother Joseph." As soon as he came to the door they drew their pistols and threatened, with many curses, to kill him. He told them to shoot, he was not afraid to die, but he demanded that they show some writ on which they made the arrest.

They had no writ to show, but they struck him with their pistols, dragged him to the wagon and tried to drive away. Stephen Markham, however, held the horses although the officers swore they would shoot him, until Emma brought Joseph's coat and hat. It was eight miles to Dixon, and on the way these bad men kept striking him and punching him in the sides with their pistols. When they reached the tavern, where they changed horses, the Prophet was almost fainting. A great spot on each side was black and blue from their blows.

Brother Markham had followed the kidnappers on horesback to Dixon, and before they could get away, he told the story of the outrage and secured a lawyer. The brutal officers were arrested and placed in charge of Sheriff Campbell, and Joseph was given a writ of habeas corpus, which permitted him to have a hearing before the circuit court at Ottawa.

Next day Joseph, in the hands of Reynolds and Wilson, and they in the hands of Sheriff Campbell, started out. They stopped at night at Pawpaw grove, where the Prophet was asked to preach. Reynolds jumped up and yelled that the people must disperse, but an old man with a thick cane walked up and said to the Missourian:

"You damned infernal puke, we'll learn you to come here and interrupt our gentleman. Sit down there, and sit still. Don't you open your heard until General Smith gets through talking. If you never learned manners in Missouri, we'll teach you that gentlemen are not to be imposed upon by a nigger-driver. You cannot kidnap men here."

Reynolds knew that he would be lynched if he did not behave, and he sat down very quietly. The Prophet spoke for an hour and a half on marriage, the subject called for by the audience.

Judge Caton of the circuit court was found to be in New York. A new writ was made out and the party started for Quincy to have the trial before Judge Douglas. Stephen Markham rode quickly on horseback toward Nauvoo, but on the way met one hundred and seventy-five men, who, hearing that the Prophet was being kidnapped, had come to rescue him.

When they met him some of them burst into tears and threw their arms about him. Joseph said to Reynolds and Wilson, "I think I will not go to Missouri this time, gentlemen, these are my boys." The two sheriffs were nearly frightened to death, thinking they were going to be punished at once, and Reynolds asked, "Is Jem Flack in the crowd?" Some on answered that the Missourian would see him the next day. With a doleful look Reynolds whined, "Then I am a dead man, for I know him of old." The Prophet, however, gave the officers his pledge that no harm should be done them.

It was decided by Joseph's lawyers and the others that the trial might be held at Nauvoo instead of Quincy and this was very pleasing to the Prophet. Reynolds and Wilson, however, kept plotting to get Joseph into the hands of his enemies. They wished to take him to the mouth of Rock river, which flowed into the Mississippi, where a band of their friends were waiting to help them, but Sheriff Campbell, who had them under arrest, took away their arms and kept them from again running away with the Prophet.

Before they reached Nauvoo one of the lawyers for the kidnappers challenged any of the party to wrestle at side-hold for a wager. Stephen Markham offered to wrestle him for fun and the lawyer threw him. Joseph's enemies, lacking the spirit of true sport, began making fun of Brother Markham and his friends. The Prophet turned to Philemon C. Merrill, a young man, and said, "Get up and throw that man."

Brother Merrill was not a side-hold wrestler and he hesitated, but Joseph again commanded him in such a tone that the young man waited to offer no excuse. He stood up, held up his arms and told the lawyer to choose his hold. He did not object when his opponent put his right arm under. The Prophet said: "Philemon, when I count three, throw him." As soon as the signal was given, Brother Merrill swung the lawyer over his shoulder and threw him, head downward, to the ground. All who saw the act were filled with awe.

At Nauvoo all was gladness at the Prophet's safe return. Hyrum took his brother in his arms and wept for joy. A feast was prepared at the Prophet's house and Reynolds and Wilson with about fifty others sat down at the table. Emma entertained these men who had tried to kidnap and murder her husband, as if they were guests of honor, but so brutal had they become that when they left Nauvoo they went to Carthage and tried to raise the militia to come upon the city of the Saints. This Governor Ford was wise enough to refuse. Joseph was set free by the court at Nauvoo, and for a time his troubles were at an end.

CHAPTER XXXVII.

1843-1844.

THE last time of peace in the life of the Prophet Joseph Smith had come, and even this peace was broken by the mutterings of a storm that was about to break upon him and crush out his dear life. At this time Joseph was as complete a man, and his life was as nearly perfect, as can be found among mortal men in all the history of this world. He had an almost fault-less body. He was full of physical strength and courage and possessed the best of health. His mind was great and vigorous. He had a broader view of politics and philosophy than the deepest politicians and philosophers of the world. He was living near unto God, and enjoyed the presence of that best companion, the Holy Ghost. He felt that his end was near and this seemed to raise him above the conditions and weaknesses of mortal men. He had so many exalted thoughts and doctrines to teach the Saints, and he strove so hard to make them understand! Oh, his life was indeed beautiful!

There were many things that saddened these last few months. Meetings were held by his enemies to rouse the spirit of hate against him, but more serious and more sorrowful was the fall of some of the men who had been his dear friends and companions. Wilson Law, who only a short time before had spoken burning words of truth in defense of Joseph, having given way to temptation, lost his former love and became a bitter enemy. William Law, Francis and Chauncey Higbee, Robert and Charles Foster, followed the same course. Even Sidney Rigdon lost the spirit of the Gospel and would have been rejected by the Saints, if Hyrum had not pleaded for mercy. Joseph knew too well Sidney's true condition, and no longer gave him his trust and confidence.

Early Christmas morning of 1843, Joseph and Hyrum awoke thinking they heard the sweet singing of angels. The song was, "Mortals awake, with angels join." They rose from their bed, and, going to the window saw below them in the hazy light of dawn, a group of men and women who were singing this Christmas carol. The melody filled their hearts with tenderness and joy, and after the song was ended, Joseph pronounced a blessing upon the singers. That same Christmas day, Orrin Porter Rockwell, with long hair, looking rough and wild, appeared among the company gathered at the Prophet's home. He had been set free from the Missouri prison and came away honorably as the Prophet had prophesied. He told a thrilling story of his adventures, and one little circumstance he related shows his character.

Knowing that Joseph had great confidence in Porter, Reynolds had tried to persuade him to go and lead the Prophet into a trap so that the Missourians could catch him. They promised Brother Rockwell great rewards and safety—almost anything he wished if he would but act as the traitor. Reynolds said to him,

"You only deliver Joe Smith into our hands and name your pile." But Porter replied, "I will see you all damned first, and then I won't."

In the spring of 1844, many leading men asked Joseph to permit them to name him as a candidate for the presidency of the United States. After much thought and prayer he consented, and on the twenty-ninth of January, he was nominated at Nauvoo. One week later he wrote an address to the people of the United States, giving his ideas of what the President and Congress should do. He was not the choice of either the Democratic or Whig party, but he had principles of his own that were far in advance of the politics of that day. He declared that slavery was wrong, but said that the slaves should be bought and set free by the government. Just think of the millions of lives that would have been saved and the millions of dollars, also, if his plan for the freedom of the slaves had been accepted! In the spring some of the Apostles and many of the Elders went out to the states to speak in favor of Joseph's election.

While the Prophet was working for peace in the nation and working for peace toward the Saints, his enemies were holding meetings to plan for his destruction. One of these was as Carthage, on the seventeenth of February, the very day that Joseph sent out an appeal to the good people of the state for peace. The meeting was made up of men whose later actions showed that they were willing to murder in order to do away with the Prophet, and yet they appointed, awful as it was, a day for fasting and prayer, thinking no doubt, that this would make their bloody work appear as righteousness to the world.

You remember a short time before this Joseph had prophesied that the Saints would go to the Rocky mountains, and there become a mighty people. When he saw trouble gathering, his mind turned toward the West. He directed the exploring parties to prepare themselves and go out to look for a suitable resting place for the Saints, when their next move should come. In civilization there seemed no rest for them. Many times he referred to the subject and directed the Apostles to secure strong, prudent men and send them out. Many volunteered and prepared themselves to go.

Joseph at this time prophesied that within five years the Saints should be out of the power of mobs and apostates. He did not live to see this fulfilled, but you know how true the prophecy was. By February of 1849, five years from the time that the Prophet uttered it, the body of the Church was in Salt Lake valley, one thousand miles from their old persecutors.

A special conference of the Church was held at Nauvoo, beginning the sixth of April, 1844. The seventh was Sunday, and twenty thousand Saints gathered to hear the Prophet speak. Elder King Follett, a faithful man who had been in prison with Parley P. Pratt in Missouri, had died a few days before, and Joseph's mind was drawn to the eternal glory that this man and other faithful Saints will obtain. For three and a half hours, in power rested the Holy Ghost upon him and he spoke. His voice was like the voice of an angel, and the people sat motionless, almost breathless, listening to hear every word.

The Laws and Fosters could no longer hide their wickedness and they were publicly cut off the Church. Now began their lawless, murderous course. Before the week had passed a number of them were arrested and fined for assault and resisting officers of the law. Joseph was determined that they should not deceive innocent Saints, and before they were cut off he

laid open their wickedness in public, and their thirst for
his blood grew stronger within them.   William Law
and others went to Carthage and swore to a complaint
before the circuit court, charging the Prophet with
polygamy and perjury.

Joseph heard that an order for his arrest was out,
and so on the twenty-fifth of May, he went of his own
free will to Carthage to give himself up.   He obtained
lawyers there and wished to have the case tried at once,
but the other side succeeded in having it delayed until
the next term of court.   Joseph was left in the hands
of a sheriff, who knowing the Prophet's honor let him
go free.   He learned from some of the apostates, who
were not so bitter as others, that a plot had been formed
to murder him that night at Carthage.   Hyrum and
others of his friends were with him, and when the mob
was not expecting it, they left Carthage and went
rapidly toward Nauvoo.   Joseph rode his favorite
horse, a beautiful animal which he called Joe Duncan.
They reached home soon after dark by rapid riding.

CHAPTER XXXVIII.

1844.

THE PLOT OF AN APOSTATE—THE PUBLICATION OF THE
NAUVOO "EXPOSITOR"—DECLARED A NUISANCE AND
ABATED AS SUCH—JOSEPH'S LAST PUBLIC SPEECH—
HE AND HIS BROTHER HYRUM LEAVE NAUVOO—RE-
TURN TO THE CITY—"I AM GOING LIKE A LAMB TO
THE SLAUGHTER."

THE mutterings of that storm of hatred, lies and
murder changed to the storm itself when the *Nauvoo Expositor* came out on the seventh of June, 1844.
It was a weekly newspaper printed by the Laws, Hig-

bees and Fosters, and was filled with the apostate spirit. Joseph and Hyrum were the main objects of its lying attacks. It also urged that the charter of Nauvoo be withdrawn on account of the fraud and crimes which, it said, were practiced under it. On this same day Robert Foster came to the Prophet and asked to see him alone, saying he wished to come back into the Church. Joseph refused to see him without witnesses, and as they spoke he pointed to Foster's breast and said, "What have you concealed there?" Foster confessed it was his pistol, and after a few more words, left the house, promising to come back, but he never came. It was soon learned that he had wished to draw Joseph off alone and then murder him.

Three days after the *Expositor* came out, the city council met and decided that this paper was a public nuisance, and, as in ordinary cases, Marshal John P. Greene was directed to remove it. Taking a number of men with him as assistants, he quietly went to the office, took the press out of the building, broke it and pied the type. Joseph, as mayor of the city, made a proclamation telling why this action had been taken. It was simply self-protection. If the *Nauvoo Expositor* had gone on, sooner or later mobs would have come upon Nauvoo, and the city would have suffered the terrible fate of Far West.

The publishers hurried to Carthage and told their story. Constable David Bettisworth was sent to arrest Joseph and Hyrum Smith and the others who had been concerned in destroying the *Expositor*. Thomas Morrison, justice of the peace at Carthage, had issued a warrant and had directed the officers to bring the prisoners before him or some other justice of the peace within the county. Joseph and Hyrum asked that they be taken before a justice of the peace in Nauvoo, but the constable said. "I will be damned but I will

carry you before Justice Morrison at Carthage." The
brethren therefore obtained a writ of habeas corpus
from the city court of Nauvoo and after being examined
were set free.

Though Marshal Greene's action had been perfectly lawful and regular, it was a somewhat unusual
thing to do, and Joseph sent a statement to Governor
Ford when the excitement began to rise, telling plainly
the whole affair and offering to go to Springfield, the
capital of Illinois, to be tried by any court that could
properly try the case.   Judge Thomas came to Nauvoo
on the sixteenth and counseled Marshal Greene, Joseph,
Hyrum, John Taylor and the others who had taken part
in destroying the press, to go before a justice of the
peace and be tried for the offense, saying that if they
were acquitted, he would be bound to make the mob
keep the peace.   They went before Daniel H. Wells,
who was not then a member of the Church, and after
a full, careful trial, were set free, Esquire Wells decid-
ing that they were not guilty.

On the very day that this trial was held mobs
began to gather.   Hundreds poured over the Mississippi river to have a hand in what they thought would
be bloody work, and the worst characters in the sur-
rounding country gathered, with muskets and cannon,
to attack Nauvoo.   As commanding officer of the
Nauvoo Legion, Joseph ordered his men to arms and
declared the city under martial law.   He stood upon the
platform in full uniform and spoke to his soldiers and
the Saints.   It was his last public address.   As he spoke
he drew his sword and stretched his arm toward heaven,
and standing there in the splendor of his manhood, he
uttered these words:

I call God and angels to witness that I have unsheathed
my sword with a firm and unalterable determination
that this people shall have their legal rights, and be

protected from mob violence, or my blood shall be spilt upon the ground like water, and my body consigned to the silent tomb.

About this time the Prophet told a dream that he had had. He was riding in a carriage with his guardian angel, and at the roadside he saw two snakes coiled up together. The angel explained that these were Robert Foster and Chauncey Higbee. Farther on William and Wilson Law dragged him from his carriage, and after binding his hands, threw him into a deep pit. Terrible beasts then fell upon Wilson, and a serpent coiled itself about William and they cried, "O, Brother Joseph, Brother Joseph, save us or we perish!" He told them that they had bound him and thrown him into a pit and he could not help them. Then his angel came and said, "Joseph, why are you here?" He replied, "Mine enemies fell upon me and bound me and threw me into this pit." The angel took him by the hand, drew him up, and they went on together.

Governor Ford came into Carthage three days after the Nauvoo Legion had been called out, and at once sent to Joseph asking that a committee of discreet men be sent to him from Nauvoo. Apostle John Taylor and Dr. John M. Bernhisel, after hastily gathering a number of papers, set out to lay the true condition of things before the governor. He talked with them and read aloud their written statements while in the company of the worst enemies of the Church, who continually interrupted him with oaths and threats. He plainly showed that he was too weak, or at least unwilling to enforce the law. When Joseph and Hyrum learned this they knew their only course to save Nauvoo, without giving themselves up to slaughter, was to flee.

On the night of the twenty-second of June, while the tears were flowing fast from their eyes, Joseph and

Hyrum, in company with Willard Richards, bade farewell to their families and Nauvoo and crossed the Mississippi river. Orrin P. Rockwell rowed them over in a leaky skiff, and on the way they used their boots and shoes to bale out the water to keep from sinking. On the next morning they began to prepare actively for their journey westward, having decided that they would go to the Rocky mountains, knowing that if they were absent from Nauvoo the mob would not attack the city.

As they were thus working, word came from Emma and many of those who had pretended great friendship, asking Joseph to return to Nauvoo, insinuating that he was a coward and was running from danger. Joseph and Hyrum were men that could not bear this reproach. They at once set out for home, and as they went Joseph said, "We are going back to be butchered." Hyrum replied, "If we live or die, we will be reconciled to our fate." As they walked to the river bank, Joseph, deep in thought, fell behind, and some one called to him to hasten. He looked up and said, "There is time enough for the slaughter."

Next morning, Joseph, with the seventeen others for whom the order of arrest had first been made, started for Carthage. As they passed the temple the Prophet gazed upon it and looked over the city, then in a tender, sad tone he said to his companions: "This is the loveliest place and these are the best people under the heavens; little do they know the trials that await them." On their way they met Captain Dunn with sixty troopers from Carthage. He had an order for the state arms held by the Nauvoo Legion, from Governor Ford, and Joseph, as lieutenant-general, signed this at his request. After this act the Prophet said to those about him:

"I am going like a lamb to the slaughter, but I am

calm as a summer's morning. I have a conscience void of offense toward God and toward all men. If they take my life I shall die an innocent man, and my blood shall cry from the ground for vengeance, and it shall yet be said of me, 'He was murdered in cold blood.' "

Dunn feared to go to Nauvoo on the brutal errand of the governor, and asked Joseph to go with him so that he might be safe. Though the brethren were loth to give up their arms, fearing a repetition of Independence and Far West, yet they had such faith in the Prophet's command that they obeyed. These, you remember, were state arms and the governor had a right according to law to demand them, though he was a coward for doing so. Their obedience shows how willing the Saints were to obey the law. Again bidding farewell, Joseph and Hyrum turned away and left Nauvoo forever.

CHAPTER XXXIX.

1844.

UNDER THE GOVERNOR'S PLEDGE OF PROTECTION JOSEPH
AND HIS BRETHREN GO TO CARTHAGE—ARRESTED
AND IMPRISONED—OCCURRENCES AT CARTHAGE—
PLOT TO MURDER THE PROPHET—GOVERNOR FORD'S
COWARDICE AND TREACHERY.

THE departure from Nauvoo was the beginning of the end. The brethren reached Carthage about midnight, and found the mob awaiting them. As they came up, a flood of threats and curses poured out from the drunken rabble. Governor Ford, hearing this, put hs head out of the window and begged the mob to go quietly to their quarters, promising to exhibit the prisoners in the morning. They spent the rest of the night at an inn where they found a number of apostates, who said openly that the intention was to kill them.

Early next morning they gave themselves up to Constable Bettisworth, who had made the arrest at

THE NAUVOO MANSION.

Nauvoo, and then went to see the governor. He had sent word to them before they reached Carthage that they would be protected from harm, and now he gave his word and promised as governor of Illinois that they should have protection and a fair trial. When the visit was over Ford took them before the mob militia and introduced the Prophet and Hyrum as Generals Joseph and Hyrum Smith. The Carthage Greys threw up their hats, drew their swords and yelled, "We will introduce ourselves to the damned 'Mormons' in a different style." Ford answered, "You shall have the full satisfaction." Soon after, the Greys were put under guard for mutiny, but were at once set free.

When the brethren returned to the tavern from their visit to the governor, the leaders of the mob called on Joseph. They confessed he did not look like a desperate man, but said that they could not see his heart. He answered that he could see their hearts, that they were filled with murder. He prophesied to them that they should see scenes of blood and horror to their hearts' content. Many should face the cannon's mouth and endure all the evil they knew of.

The brethren had come to Carthage to be tried before Justice Morrison on the charge of riot, because he had issued the order for their arrest and the governor was not satisfied to accept the judgment of Daniel H. Wells or any other justice. But now in the afternoon of the twenty-fifth they were brought before Robert F. Smith, who was also captain of the Carthage Greys and a more bitter enemy than Morrison. The brethren were released on seven thousand five hundred dollar bonds.

That morning Joseph and Hyrum had been arrested for treason and at night the constable came with an order from Smith to take them to prison. Their lawyers refused to permit them to go, since the action was illegal, and Smith applied to the governor for advice. Ford said, "You have the Carthage Greys at your command." The justice of the peace, seeing the point, went with his men and dragged Joseph and Hyrum to prison.

The night was spent in prayer by the prisoners and the brethren who had gone with them. Next morning, on Joseph's written request, Governor Ford came, and Joseph had a long talk with him. The Prophet explained the whole situation, and Ford seemed perfectly satisfied. He pledged the honor of himself and his officers to give the Prophet protection and he prom-

HYRUM SMITH'S RESIDENCE.

ised that if he went to Nauvoo the following day, he would take him back.

After Ford left, the brethren took turns in preaching to the guards. Several times they were changed because the men refused to take any part in doing such a terrible wrong to those whom they had grown certain were innocent. At half past two in the afternoon the jailor refused to give up the prisoners on the order from Justice Smith, as Smith had no authority to demand them. Once more the governor advised the use of the Carthage Greys in place of law, and the prisoners were forcibly taken into court. The charge was treason, and for a long time Justice Smith refused to have witnesses from Nauvoo, but at length the trial was put off until the twenty-ninth of June, three days later.

When they went back to prison that night, Hyrum, who seemed far mare hopeful than Joseph, read from the Book of Mormon comforting passages that told how God in marvelous ways had delievered His servants. The Prophet then bore his testimony in great power to the guards concerning the truth of the Gospel, and late at night the prisoners lay down to sleep. After a time Joseph whispered to Dan Jones who was lying beside him, "Are you afraid to die?" and Brother Jones replied, "Has that time come, think you? Engaged in such a cause, I do not think that death would have many terrors." Then the Prophet whispered, "You will yet see Wales and fulfill the mission appointed you, before you die." Next morning Brother Jones left the prison to learn the cause of a disorder outside during the night. Frank Worrel, one of the Carthage Greys, said:

"We have had too much trouble to bring old Joe here to let him escape alive, and unless you want to die with him, you had better leave before sundown; and you are not a damned bit better than him for taking his part, and you'll see that I can prophesy better than old Joe, for neither he nor his brother, nor anyone else who will remain with them, will see the sun set today."

As Brother Jones went on he learned positively that the Carthage Greys and others of the mob intended to kill the prisoners that day. He hurried to the governor and found that Ford had decided to go to Nauvoo, taking the best troops with him and leaving the prisoners in the hands of the mob. He would not listen to what Brother Jones said, and even refused to allow any of the Prophet's friends who were outside the jail to go back, nor Apostles Taylor and Richards, who were inside, to come out. Brother Jones went away and soon returned with Cyrus H. Wheelock and John P. Greene. They urged the governor to remember his promise and not leave those whom he had pledged the honor of the state to protect, to be murdered in cold blood; but Ford was too great a coward to disappoint the mob. He set out for Nauvoo.

Perhaps the governor did not know for certain that the plot was to kill the prisoners during his absence, and yet he knew the danger they were in, for he said in his speech to the Saints:

"A great crime has been done by destroying the *Expositor* press, and placing the city under martial law, and a severe atonement must be made, so prepare your minds for the emergency."

This was the afternoon, and as he spoke, a cannon in the distance was heard. One of his aids whispered something in his ear, and immediately the governor with his officers and the troops rode away as though in fear. It was probably the cannon fired near Carthage as a signal that the mob had been successful in its foul work. While at Nauvoo during the day, Ford and his friends had gone into the Temple, and some amused themselves by breaking the horns off the oxen that held up the baptismal font, and the officers were heard to say time after time that the Prophet would die that day.

CHAPTER XL.
1844.

THE PRISONERS IN CARTHAGE JAIL—SURROUNDED BY A
MOB WITH PAINTED FACES—THE MARTYRDOM—
THE RETURN TO NAUVOO—FUNERAL AND BURIAL—
CONCLUSION.

WHEN Governor Ford left Carthage on the morning of the twenty-seventh of June, taking with him the friendly troops of Captain Dunn, he disbanded all but the Carthage Greys, and left them to guard the prison. Two hundred of the disbanded soldiers, with blackened faces came to make the attack. When all was ready, the eight men at the door of the jail loaded their muskets with blank cartridges and waited.

The four prisoners, Joseph and Hyrum Smith, John Taylor and Willard Richards, spent a very dull, gloomy day, seemingly weighed down by the terrible fate before them. In the afternoon, Brother Taylor sang this beautiful hymn:

> A poor wayfaring man of grief
>   Hath often crossed me on my way,
> Who sued so humbly for relief
>   That I could never answer nay.
> I had not power to ask his name;
> Whither he went or whence he came;
> Yet there was something in his eye
> That won my love, I knew not why.
>
> Once, when my scanty meal was spread,
>   He entered—not a word he spake!
> Just perishing for want of bread,
>   I gave him all; he blessed it, brake,
> And ate, but gave me part again;
> Mine was an angel's portion then,
> For while I fed with eager haste,
> The crust was manna to my taste

I spied him where a fountain burst
    Clear from the rock—his strength was gone
The heedless water mocked his thirst,
    He heard it, saw it hurrying on.
I ran and rais'd the suff'rer up;
Thrice from the stream he drain'd my cup,
Dipped and return'd it running o'er;
I drank, and never thirsted more.

'Twas night; the floods were out, it blew
    A winter hurricane aloof;
I heard his voice, abroad, and flew
    To bid him welcome to my roof.
I warm'd, I cloth'd, I cheered my guest,
I laid him on my couch to rest:
Then made the earth my bed, and seem'd
In Eden's garden while I dream'd

Stripp'd, wounded. beaten nigh to death,
    I found him by the highway side;
I rous'd his pulse, brought back his breath,
    Reviv'd his spirit, and supplied
Wine, oil, refreshment—he was heal'd,
I had myself a wound conceal'd;
But from that hour forgot the smart,
And peace bound up my broken heart.

In prison I saw him next—condemn'd
    To meet a traitor's doom at morn,
The tide of lying tongues I stemm'd,
    And honor'd him 'mid shame and scorn
My friendship's utmost zeal to try.
He asked if I for him would die;
The flesh was weak, my blood ran chill,
But the free spirit cried, "I will!"

Then in a moment to my view.
    The stranger started from disguise;
The tokens in his hands I knew,
    The Savior stood before mine eyes
He spake—and my poor name he nam'd—
"Of me thou hast not been ashamed;
These deeds shall thy memorial be:
Fear not, thou didst them unto me"

After this sweet song was ended the Prophet asked him to repeat it. He said that he had not the spirit of singing, but they urged him and he sang it again.

Shortly after five o'clock some of the brethren saw men with painted faces running around the corner of the jail toward the stairs. There was a cry of surrender. Three or four gun shots were heard, and in a moment the mob was at the door. The brethren placed their bodies against it and held it shut. A pistol bullet was fired into the keyhole to break the lock. Hyrum stepped back and a bullet through the door panel struck him in the face, and two bullets through the window at the same moment tore his flesh. He fell saying:
"I am a dead man."

The door was forced open and gun barrels were thrust through. Joseph fired three shots into the hallway from a pistol that had been left with him by Brother Wheelock. Brothers Taylor and Richards with heavy walking canes, tried to beat down the guns. The muskets belched great flashes of fire into the room, and it seemed that in a moment they would all be destroyed. John Taylor sprang to the window, but a bullet from the door pierced his thigh and he fell on the sill. He was slipping out head first when another bullet from the outside struck his watch and drove his body back into the room. To save himself, he began to crawl under the bed, when three other bullets splashed his blood upon the walls.

Joseph saw his brother Hyrum dead on the floor and John Taylor apparently dying. Willard Richards was still unharmed, and to save him, the Prophet ran to the window intending to spring out. While he stood for just an instant before making the leap, two bullets struck him from behind, and one bullet from the mob below. His dying words were:
"Oh Lord, my God!"

He smiled and fell to the ground—dead.

A hatless Missourian with bare legs and arms, ran to him and set his body in a sitting position against the curb of a well. Colonel Levi Williams ordered four men to shoot. They fired their bullets into the Prophet's body, but he was past the power of men to hurt. The ruffian who had placed the body against the curb, with gleaming knife in his hand rushed to cut off the

PRESIDENT JOHN TAYLOR.

head and thus gain the reward offered by enemies in
Missouri. Suddenly a light from heaven burst upon
the scene, the knife fell to the ground, and the Missourian and the four men that had shot Joseph were as
if turned to stone. The mob in terror fled on all sides,
but Williams called them to take away their four companions. They threw these into the wagon and then
set off.

Willard Richards had suffered only a slight wound
in the ear, and after hiding Brother Taylor under an
old mattress in another cell, he went out to learn
whether the Prophet was really dead or not. Though
he thought the mob would kill him, he determined to
find out Joseph's fate. He came back and told the
awful news to Apostle Taylor, and a dull, lonely, sickening pain, more terrible than the pain from his
wounds, came over that faithful man. Doctor Richards
prepared the bodies of the Prophet and Patriarch, and
early next morning, after providing for Brother Taylor, started for Nauvoo.

Thousands of weeping Saints met the sorrowful
procession. The bodies were taken at once to Joseph's
home and arranged for burial. Apostle Richards and
Colonel Stephen Markham and others spoke to the
Saints, telling them that vengeance belonged to God,
and exhorting them to remain at peace. Next morning the doors were opened and ten thousand Saints
passed by the coffin of the martyrs and looked upon
their beloved faces. At night the funeral was held,
but bags of sand were placed in the rough pine boxes
where the caskets had been, and these were buried.
At midnight the bodies were carried by ten of the brethren and were secretly buried under the foundation of
the Nauvoo House, from which place at a later time
they were moved and again buried. This secrecy was

necessary for fear of those who would have robbed the graves.

And this is the life and death of the man who was chosen, when the foundations of the world were laid, to stand next to Jesus Christ, the Only Begotten, in the importance of His work here upon the earth. God took him in his youth and trained him in His own school. He

CARTHAGE JAIL.

was a mortal man, but how splendid was his manhood, how glorious his mortality! Like the Master, he died young, but like His also were the mighty works he performed in that life. He died as he had lived, the type of highest love. He offered his life for his friends, and sealed his testimony with his blood.